# CIVIL WAR CAMPAIGNS AND COMMANDERS SERIES

Under the General Editorship of Grady McWhiney

PUBLISHED

# Jefferson Davis's Greatest General
## Albert Sidney Johnston

**Cataloging-in-Publication Data**

Roland, Charles Pierce, 1918-
   Jefferson Davis's greatest general: Albert Sidney Johnston /
    Charles P. Roland.
   p.cm.—(Civil War campaigns and commanders series)
   Includes bibliographical references and index.
   ISBN 1-893114-21-X (hrd)

   1. Johnston, Albert Sidney, 1803-1862. 2. Generals—
Confederate States of America—Biography. 3. Confederate States of
America. Army—Biography. 4. United States—History—Civil War,
1861–1865—Campaigns. 5. Shiloh, Battle of, 1862. I. Title. II. Series.

    E467.1.J73 R58  2000
    355'.0092—dc21       99-056314
                 CIP

McMurry Station, Box 637
Abilene, TX  79697-0637

Printed in the United States of America

ISBN 1-893114-21-X
10 9 8 7 6 5 4 3 2 1

Book Designed by Rosenbohm Graphic Design

All inquiries regarding volume purchases of this book should be
addressed to McWhiney Foundation Press, McMurry Station, Box 637,
Abilene, TX  79697-0637.
Telephone inquiries may be made by calling (915) 793-4682

A NOTE ON THE SERIES

Few segments of America's past excite more interest than Civil War battles and leaders. This ongoing series of brief, lively, and authoritative books–*Civil War Campaigns and Commanders*–salutes this passion with inexpensive and accurate accounts that are readable in a sitting. Each volume, separate and complete in itself, nevertheless conveys the agony, glory, death, and wreckage that defined America's greatest tragedy.

In this series, designed for Civil War enthusiasts as well as the newly recruited, emphasis is on telling good stories. Photographs and biographical sketches enhance the narrative of each book, and maps depict events as they happened. Sound history is meshed with the dramatic in a format that is just lengthy enough to inform and yet satisfy.

Grady McWhiney
General Editor

# PUBLISHER'S NOTE

On the publication of this, the twentieth title in our Civil War Campaigns and Commanders series, we wish to acknowledge some of the many people who have made this ground-breaking series such a success. General Editor and renowned Civil War historian Grady McWhiney and Senior Project Editor Drake Bush created this series in 1995. From the beginning a group of dedicated people have worked to produce a quality product that continues to evolve as new enhancements are added. This group includes Editorial Assistant Mary Bush, book designer Henry Rosenbohm of Rosenbohm Graphic Design, cartographer Donald S. Frazier, whose maps appear in each volume, and Managing Editor David Coffey, who has contributed dozens of biographical sketches over the years and now oversees series production.

The series has received significant contributions from a number of talented people, including photograph researcher Jim Enos, copy editor Gavin Lewis, editorial assistant Paul Cochran, and many others along the way.

We wish to thank President Robert Shimp and Vice President Paul Lack of McMurry University in Abilene, Texas, for their generous support of our operation. We are grateful to the fine folks at Texas A&M University Press, who market our titles through their excellent publishing consortium. And, special thanks to our many gifted authors for their talent and patience, and for making this series come to life.

Finally, thanks to you, the readers, who have supported this series from the start. Your interest, your enthusiasm, and your suggestions mean so much. We hope you enjoy this twentieth title.

We dedicate this volume to our author and friend, Dr. Lawrence Clayton.

# CONTENTS

# CAMPAIGNS AND COMMANDERS SERIES

## Map Key

### *Geography*

 Trees

 Marsh

 Fields

 Strategic Elevations

 Rivers

 Tactical Elevations

 Fords

 Orchards

 Political Boundaries

### *Human Construction*

 Bridges

 Railroads

 Tactical Towns

 Strategic Towns

 Buildings

Church

Roads

### *Military*

 Union Infantry

 Confederate Infantry

 Cavalry

 Artillery

Headquarters

 Encampments

 Fortifications

 Permanant Works

 Hasty Works

Obstructions

Engagements

 Warships

 Gunboats

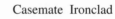 Casemate Ironclad

 Monitor

 Tactical Movements

Strategic Movements

*Maps by*
*Donald S. Frazier, Ph.D.*
*Abilene, Texas*

# MAPS

# PHOTOGRAPHS AND ILLUSTRATIONS

# Jefferson Davis's Greatest General
## Albert Sidney Johnston

Charles P. Roland

For Tom Dallanis,
"With my warm regards,"
Charles P. Roland
Jan, 25, 2001

**MCWHINEY FOUNDATION PRESS**
MCMURRY UNIVERSITY
ABILENE, TEXAS

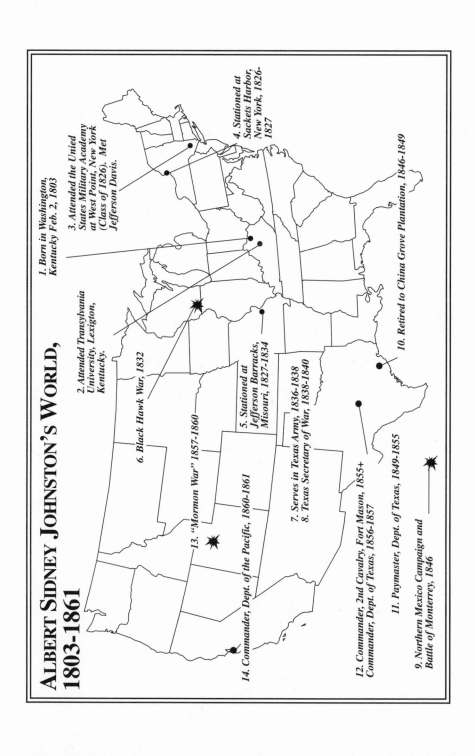

# ALBERT SIDNEY JOHNSTON'S WORLD, 1803-1861

1. Born in Washington, Kentucky Feb. 2, 1803

2. Attended Transylvania University, Lexington, Kentucky.

3. Attended the United States Military Academy at West Point, New York (Class of 1826). Met Jefferson Davis.

4. Stationed at Sackets Harbor, New York, 1826-1827

5. Stationed at Jefferson Barracks, Missouri, 1827-1834

6. Black Hawk War, 1832

7. Serves in Texas Army, 1836-1838

8. Texas Secretary of War, 1838-1840

9. Northern Mexico Campaign and Battle of Monterrey, 1846

10. Retired to China Grove Plantation, 1846-1849

11. Paymaster, Dept. of Texas, 1849-1855

12. Commander, 2nd Cavalry, Fort Mason, 1855+ Commander, Dept. of Texas, 1856-1857

13. "Mormon War" 1857-1860

14. Commander, Dept. of the Pacific, 1860-1861

# 1
# Confederate Commander of the Western Theater

There is no mystery over why Albert Sidney Johnston held
the top rank among the field generals of the Confederacy.
President Jefferson Davis considered him to be the South's
foremost soldier. "He came," Davis would say after the war,
"and by his accession I felt strengthened, knowing that a great
support had thereby been added to the Confederate cause. . . .
I hoped and expected that I had others who would prove generals, but I knew I had one, and that was Sidney Johnston."
Davis confirmed his esteem for Johnston when Johnston suffered an early defeat in the war and a state legislative delegation petitioned the president for his dismissal. Davis replied,
"If [Johnston] is not a general we had better give up the war,
for we have no general."

The association between Davis and Johnston stretched

back to their days as cadets at the United States Military Academy. Both were natives of Kentucky and alumni of Transylvania University in Lexington. At West Point Davis admired Johnston, who was two years Davis's senior and who during his final year (class of 1826) served in the coveted position of adjutant of the corps of cadets. Both men participated in the brief but strenuous Black Hawk War that occurred in the Territory of Wisconsin during the spring and summer of

## ALBERT SIDNEY JOHNSTON

Born Kentucky 1803; after attending Transylvania University, he entered the U.S. Military Academy in 1822, graduating eighth in his 1826 class of forty-one; breveted 2d lieutenant and posted to infantry, he served on the frontier and in the 1832 Black Hawk War; in 1834 he resigned his commission to care for his dying wife; after her death he moved to revolutionist Texas; in 1837 he became senior brigadier in the new republic's army and served two years as secretary of war; during the war with Mexico, Johnston commanded a regiment of Texas volunteers and saw action at Monterrey; he reentered the U.S. Army in 1849 as a major and paymaster to the military posts in Texas; in 1855 he was promoted to colonel and given command of the new 2d Cavalry, an elite regiment that included among its officers such future Civil War generals as Robert E. Lee, George Thomas, William J. Hardee, and John Bell Hood; shortly thereafter he also assumed command of the Department of Texas; in 1857 Johnston headed an expedition to Utah to quell Mormon unrest, a difficult assignment that garnered him a brevet promotion to brigadier general; he then assumed command of the Department of the Pacific with headquarters at San Francisco, and was on duty there when his adopted home state Texas seceded from the Union; resigning his U.S. commission a second time,

1832. Johnston held the position of adjutant to Brigadier General Henry Atkinson, commander of the military forces that subdued the Indians. Whether Davis saw any combat in the affair is controversial, but he did escort Black Hawk to Jefferson Barracks, Missouri, after the fighting ended.

Johnston's career underwent many vicissitudes during the years following the Black Hawk War. In 1834 he resigned his army commission at the behest of his invalid wife, and follow-

Johnston traveled overland from California to Virginia to offer his services to the Confederacy, arriving at Richmond in August 1861; considered by many America's foremost military man, he was received warmly by his friend and fellow West Point cadet, Confederate President Jefferson Davis, who appointed him full general (ranking second only to Adjutant General Samuel Cooper in the Confederate army); given command of the Western Theater (Department No. 2), Johnston worked to hold the vast region, but the surrenders of Forts Henry and Donelson in February 1862 opened Tennessee to Federal invasion and forced a general retreat southward; after concentrating his forces at Corinth, Mississippi, Johnston in early April 1862 attacked General U.S. Grant's Federal army near Pittsburg Landing, on the Tennessee River in southwestern Tennessee; the attack surprised the Federals and promised great success, but at the height of the fighting Johnston fell wounded and bled to death on the field; General P.G.T. Beauregard suspended the attack late in the day; the next day reenforced Federal troops drove the Confederates from the field; the Battle of Shiloh was the first great contest of the war and one of the bloodiest in U.S. history. Johnston had received much criticism for the loss of Tennessee, but Davis stood by his friend. A major controversy, fueled by Beauregard and his supporters on one side and William Preston Johnston (his son) on the other, developed over Johnston's role at Shiloh and the quality of his generalship. Johnston's death early in the battle and so early in the war make an evaluation of his overall generalship impossible. Although he certainly lost more ground than he won during his brief Civil War career, at the time of his death he appeared to be on the verge of a stunning victory. General Johnston's remains were eventually removed to the Texas State Cemetery in Austin.

## JEFFERSON DAVIS

Born Kentucky 1808; attended Transylvania University; graduated U.S. Military Academy twenty-third in his class in 1828; appointed 2d lieutenant in the 1st Infantry in 1828; 1st lieutenant 1st Dragoons 1833; regimental adjutant 1833 to 1834; served on the Northwest frontier and in the Black Hawk War in 1832; resigned from the army in 1835 and eloped with Zachary Taylor's daughter, who died of malaria three months after their marriage; Davis settled in Mississippi as a planter; married Varina Howell and was elected to Congress in 1845; resigned to participate in the Mexican War; appointed colonel 1st Mississippi Volunteer Infantry in 1846; serving under Taylor, he was wounded at Buena Vista in 1847; declined appointment to brigadier general; elected senator from Mississippi in 1847; secretary of war under President Franklin Pierce from 1853 to 1857; returned to the Senate where he served on military affairs committee until his resignation in 1861; president of the Confederate States of America from 1861 to 1865; captured following the war in Georgia, he was imprisoned at Fort Monroe for two years and never brought to trial; after failing in a number of business ventures, he was a poor man during his later years, living at "Beauvoir," a house on the Gulf of Mexico given to him by an admirer; Mississippi would have sent him to the Senate, but he refused to ask for the Federal pardon without which it was impossible for him to take his seat; published *The Rise and Fall of the Confederate Government* in 1881; died in New Orleans in 1889. A biographer called Davis "a very engaging young man, fearless, generous, modest, with personal charm, and in friendship rashly loyal." His loyalty to the Southern cause also never faltered. But as a president he proved to be prideful, stiff, stubborn, often narrow-minded, unwilling to compromise. These qualities kept him from becoming a great chief executive.

ing her death a year later he migrated to the infant Republic of Texas, where he served successively as commander of the army and secretary of war. When in 1846 the United States went to war with Mexico, Johnston immediately tendered his military services. Elected colonel of a regiment of Texas volunteers, he was left without a command when presently most of the troops went home following the expiration of their enlistment period.

The most memorable experience shared by Davis and Johnston in the Mexican War occurred at the end of the Battle of Monterrey early in the conflict. Both had distinguished themselves during the fighting, Davis as the commander of a regiment of Mississippi volunteers, Johnston on the staff of General William O. Butler, a division commander. Johnston had demonstrated extraordinary courage and presence of mind in rallying a body of panicked American soldiers and turning back a charge by Mexican mounted lancers. Accompanying Davis to secure a copy of the armistice terms from the Mexican commander, Johnston extricated the two of them from a threatening situation in the enemy lines by forcing the commander's adjutant to escort them to his headquarters. Davis never forgot the incident and said of it, "[Johnston] exhibited that quick perception and decision which characterize the military genius."

Johnston languished for almost a decade after the Mexican War. During the early years of that period he worked futilely at becoming a successful planter in Texas. For the remainder of the time, having reentered the army as a major, he served in the laborious and monotonous job of paymaster to the garrisons at forts scattered across the Texas frontier. Meanwhile, in 1853 his friend and admirer Davis became Secretary of War. He did not forget Johnston. Sponsoring the creation of two new cavalry regiments to guard the western frontier against Indians, Davis was instrumental in 1855 in having Johnston appointed to the command of the 2nd Cavalry, with headquarters at Fort Mason, near the Llano River in west-central Texas.

Except for the isolation and Spartan conditions of life at the fort, Johnston held a choice assignment. The regiment was an elite unit. Indeed, Davis was suspected of packing it with his favorites. Its officer roster contained many names that would become famous on both sides in the Civil War. Besides Johnston as the commanding officer, it included Lieutenant Colonel Robert E. Lee (second-in-command), Majors William J. Hardee and George H. Thomas, Captains Earl Van Dorn, Edmund Kirby Smith, Innis N. Palmer, and George Stoneman, and Lieutenants John Bell Hood, Nathan G. Evans, Richard W. Johnson, Kenner Garrard, and Charles W. Field.

Soon Johnston was elevated to the temporary command of the entire Department of Texas in addition to his duties as a regimental commander. He conducted the affairs of the regiment and the department in such an exemplary fashion that in the summer of 1857 he was appointed by new Secretary of War John Floyd to undertake a particularly delicate mission of both military and diplomatic import. He was assigned to command an expedition to the Territory of Utah to quell the so-called Mormon Insurrection.

This turned out to be an extremely difficult and distasteful chore. After a threat of resistance in the mountain passes east of Salt Lake Valley, the Mormon military forces drew back and permitted Johnston's little army to enter their domain without serious incident. Now began a prolonged military occupation that grew steadily more demanding and monotonous. He carried out his duties faithfully and was rewarded with a brevet promotion to brigadier general. He loathed the Mormons' custom of polygamy, and he despised even more their passive but determined resistance to federal authority and their practice of what he viewed as an autocratic theocracy. He chafed under instructions from the War Department that prohibited him from the use of troops in altering Mormon affairs. He wrote to his son in frustration, complaining that his lot was worse than that of an exile to Siberia.

In January 1860 the War Department relieved Johnston from the Utah position and in November assigned him to the command of the Pacific Department, with headquarters in San Francisco. By now, the ominous cloud of secession lay over the nation. Johnston was an ardent nationalist in most respects, but his sympathies were with the South in the slavery issue. He hated the abolitionists, describing them as "fanatical, idolatrous negro worshippers," and he once said that rather than suffer their agitations the Southerners ought to abandon the Union. "We say," he wrote angrily, "away with such an union only fair to behold, but foul in its embrace." His ultimate loyalty lay with his adopted state of Texas, and when that state seceded he resigned his commission in the United States Army.

He originally intended to remain neutral and sit out the war in California. But he found himself unable to do this after hostilities actually began at Fort Sumter. His second wife later explained, "It seemed impossible in the excitement of the times for him to 'beat his sword into a ploughshare.' The two sections of the country North and South being opposed to each other and the intense bitterness of the struggle already commenced caused his sympathy for his own people, who needed every arm that could handle a gun, to influence his decision." She quoted him as saying, "It looks like fate, that Texas has made me a Rebel twice." On June 16 he left Los Angeles with a company of other Southerners who made their way through the sand and scorching heat of the Southwest to join the Confederacy. He arrived at Richmond in early September.

Davis was said to have recognized the sound of Johnston's step in the hall of the Confederate White House and ordered that he be admitted to the president's room immediately. News of Johnston's coming had preceded him; a delegation of citizens had already called upon Davis to request that he appoint Johnston to command the Western Theater of the Confederacy. Major General Leonidas Polk, once Johnston's West Point roommate and now the ranking military officer in the West, had written Davis to urge the same thing and to say, "I know of no man who has the capacity to fill the position, who could be had, but General Johnston."

Johnston seemed a perfect choice for the command of the Western Theater. Virtually everyone acquainted with his career considered him to be one of the foremost American officers of the time. A sketch published by *Harper's Weekly* magazine during the Utah affair captured him splendidly. "Johnston is now in the matured vigor of manhood. He is above six feet in height, strongly and powerfully formed, with a grave, dignified, and commanding presence. His features are strongly marked, showing his Scottish lineage, and denote great resolution and composure of character. His complexion, naturally fair, is, from exposure, a deep brown. His habits are abstemious and temperate, and no excess has impaired his powerful constitution. His mind is clear, strong, and well cultivated. His manner is courteous, but rather grave and silent. He has many devoted friends, but they have been won and secured rather by the native dignity and nobility of his character than by his powers of address. He is a man of strong will and ardent temper, but his whole bearing testifies to the self-control he has acquired."

Generals Zachary Taylor and William J. Worth, Johnston's superiors in the Mexican War, had commented that he was the finest soldier they knew. General Winfield Scott, commander of Union forces at the beginning of the Civil War, wrote of Johnston at the time of the Utah expedition, "[He] is more than a good officer. He is a God send to the country through the army." Scott was said to have favored Johnston for high command in the Union army. General U. S. Grant would write years later that the Union officers who had known Johnston before the war expected him to be the most formidable opponent they would meet on the battlefield.

Davis urgently needed a competent general for the West. Confederate forces in Virginia were under the command of Generals Joseph E. Johnston and P. G. T. Beauregard, victors of the Battle of Manassas. No officer of comparable stature was present west of the Appalachians. Albert Sidney Johnston, as a native of Kentucky and an adoptive son of Texas, and as an officer who had spent most of his career west of the Mississippi River, seemed almost a providential answer to Davis's need for the western command. Davis now proposed it and Johnston accepted it without hesitation.

On September 10 Davis issued the order that assigned Johnston to the command of Confederate Department Number Two—a broad area spreading from the Appalachians on the east through Indian Territory (the present state of Oklahoma) on the west, and including the states of Kentucky and Missouri, slave states of divided loyalty that were considered by the Confederacy to be within its authority, Tennessee and Arkansas, and the northern portions of Alabama, Mississippi, and Louisiana. Johnston was appointed a full general, ranking second only to Adjutant General Samuel Cooper, who was too old for a field command.

Johnston left immediately to take up his new duties, arriving at Nashville by train on September 14. There he enjoyed briefly a visit with his eldest child, William Preston Johnston, a Louisville lawyer who had recently been appointed a major in the Confederate army and was on his way to join his regiment in Virginia. The two were not to meet again.

Requested by the citizens of Nashville to make a public appearance, Johnston did so and addressed the meeting as "Fellow soldiers of the reserve corps." The expression drew a sympathetic response; a local editor commented, "This was a well-timed remark, and showed that, as a military man, he knew what was coming. The South will need all of her force. Every able-bodied man may as well make up his mind to it, and that soon."

The situation facing him required far more than oratory. He had to decide at once whether to deploy his meager and scattered forces in Kentucky for a determined effort to hold the

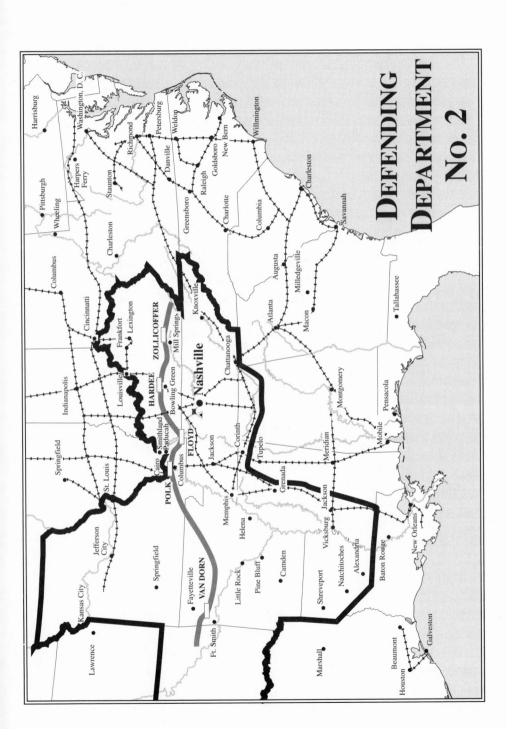

state for the Confederacy, or give up Kentucky and dispose his troops for the strongest possible defense of Tennessee. Kentucky was split in its loyalties; the state administration sought to remain neutral. But ten days before Johnston reached Nashville, General Polk had occupied Columbus, Kentucky, on the Mississippi River. Union forces promptly responded by seizing the mouths of the Tennessee and Cumberland Rivers at Paducah and Smithland.

Johnston, while en route from Virginia, had ordered Brigadier General Felix Zollicoffer with a small contingent of troops to move from Knoxville to Cumberland Ford in eastern Kentucky to secure the Cumberland Gap, which led through the mountains from Virginia. The Kentucky legislature now demanded the withdrawal of all Confederate troops.

Urged by Governor Isham Harris of Tennessee, Johnston decided on the bolder course, to establish his line in Kentucky. He pointed out to the Richmond authorities that the most defensible terrain feature north of Tennessee was the Barren River above Bowling Green, Kentucky; that to yield this line to the Federals and pull back his troops from Columbus and Cumberland Ford would lead to the loss of Kentucky and the immediate invasion of Tennessee.

He amplified his strategic reasoning by stating, "The Government of the United States appreciating the vast resources to be obtained by the subjugation of Kentucky will make its greatest efforts here for this purpose. If we could wrest this rich fringe from his grasp the war could be carried across the border and the contest speedily decided upon our own terms." Johnston's hope for a quick Confederate victory was vastly optimistic, but his analysis of the importance of Kentucky was matched by Abraham Lincoln's statement that for the Union to lose the state was "almost to lose the whole game."

On September 17, 1861 Johnston sent Brigadier General Simon Bolivar Buckner and a contingent of 4,000 soldiers by rail from Nashville to occupy Bowling Green. He then issued a proclamation to the people of Kentucky, advising them that he had sent Confederate troops into Kentucky in response to the presence of Union forces there, and that he was willing to withdraw his own men if Union authorities would do the same. The people of the state might, if they chose, resume their neutrality, or they might join either the Confederacy or the Union. But if they should decide to fight with the Union, he said, then none

## SIMON BOLIVAR BUCKNER

Born Kentucky 1823; graduated U.S. Military Academy 1844, eleventh in his class of twenty-five; brevetted 2d lieutenant of infantry, he saw duty on the frontier and taught at West Point; promoted to 2d lieutenant in 1846, he joined General Winfield Scott's command in Mexico, where he was wounded at Churubusco and won brevet promotions to 1st lieutenant and captain; returned briefly to West Point as an instructor in infantry tactics; promoted to 1st lieutenant in 1851 and received the staff rank of captain in 1852; the bulk of his service was on the Western frontier until his resignation from the Army in 1855; Buckner engaged in real estate with his father-in-law in Chicago and managed his wife's substantial holdings; in 1858 settled in Louisville; active in the Kentucky militia, becoming inspector general in 1860; with the coming of the Civil War he worked to secure Kentucky's neutrality, declining a Federal brigadier general's commission proffered by President Abraham Lincoln and General Scott; although Buckner owned no slaves and opposed secession, he opted for the Confederacy following pro-Union posturing in the state legislature; appointed brigadier general in Confederate service in September 1861, he led a force that occupied Bowling Green, Kentucky, shortly thereafter; in February 1862, after senior officers J.B. Floyd and G.J. Pillow fled, Buckner surrendered

could doubt the right of the Confederates to enter the state.

The occupation of Bowling Green created a trace of a defensive line for Johnston's department. But it was a ragged and irregular line that featured many large and dangerous gaps. Indeed, in most places it was nothing more than an outpost line. More alarming than the gaps, the line was penetrated by three major rivers, the Mississippi, Tennessee, and

Fort Donelson to his friend and West Point classmate U.S. Grant; imprisoned in Massachusetts until exchanged in August 1862; promoted to major general, he joined the Army of Tennessee; led a division in General Braxton Bragg's Kentucky invasion; given command of the District of the Gulf in December 1862 and the Department of East Tennessee in May 1863; rejoined Bragg's army and led a corps in General James Longstreet's Wing in the victory at Chickamauga; following that battle, Buckner joined a group of officers who called for Bragg's removal and may have penned the petition that many high-ranking generals signed; Bragg retaliated by reducing Buckner to division command and abolishing his Department of East Tennessee; a long illness kept Buckner from active duty until the spring of 1864; he served on the court martial of General Lafayette McLaws and declined the command of General J.B. Hood's former Army of Northern Virginia Division; transferred to the Trans-Mississippi and promoted to lieutenant general in September 1864, Buckner commanded the District of West Louisiana, served as chief of staff for General E. Kirby Smith, and surrendered along with Smith at New Orleans in May 1865; forbidden to leave Louisiana, Buckner worked as a commission merchant and newspaperman until allowed to return to Kentucky in 1868; able to recover his confiscated property in Kentucky and Chicago, he purchased the Louisville *Courier* and served as its editor for twenty years; governor of Kentucky from 1887 to 1892, vice presidential candidate on the "Gold Democrat" ticket in 1896, General Buckner died at his estate near Munfordville in 1914, the last surviving Confederate general above the grade of brigadier. Although he saw limited combat, Buckner performed capably when given the opportunity. His involvement in the anti-Bragg faction no doubt damaged his career.

Cumberland, all linked to the Ohio a short distance behind the Union front. The town of Cairo, Illinois, located at the junction of the Ohio with the Mississippi, was an important pivot point from which Federal forces could be moved with dispatch against various parts of the Confederate line.

Johnston was keenly aware of the line's weakness. He commanded fewer than 40,000 troops against a foe of half again this number led by Johnston's former West Point classmate and friend, Major General Robert Anderson. Johnston hoped to enlist sufficient additional soldiers from within his department to enable him to hold the line or possibly launch an attack. Meanwhile, he sought to protect his area by acting as if his force were much stronger than it actually was. He instructed his subordinates to maneuver their troops as if they were preparing to move forward. Reconnaissance and raiding parties were to create the impression that his entire force was only the advance guard of a great army.

The left flank of Johnston's Kentucky line was anchored at Columbus and under the command of General Polk. Polk had left the old army shortly after his graduation from the Military Academy. Embarking on a career as an Episcopal clergyman, he eventually rose to be the bishop of Louisiana. From this position he entered the Confederate army. Johnston established the center of his Kentucky line at Bowling Green, and concentrated his major force there, with his former Second Cavalry subordinate Major General William J. Hardee in command. Zollicoffer's light force at Cumberland Ford held the extreme right of the line. Also within Johnston's theater was a small force in western Arkansas, which shortly would be placed under the command of another of his former subordinates, Brigadier General Earl Van Dorn.

Johnston attempted to strengthen his forces by calling upon the governors of the states within his theater for additional levies of troops. He appealed also to the Confederate government in Richmond, pointing out vigorously the importance of the Mississippi Valley and predicting that the Federals would use their control of the rivers to attack him, that they rightly understood that his region was the "seat of vitality" of the Confederacy, and would muster all of their strength to seize it. In January 1862 he wrote to the Confederate Adjutant General: "All the resources of the Confederacy are now needed for the defence [sic] of Tennessee."

Johnston organized his military staff along conventional lines, with a department of orders, a quartermaster department, and an engineer corps. Though he had no chief of staff, his assistant adjutant general, Lieutenant Colonel W.W. Mackall, who had served him in the same capacity when he commanded the Department of the Pacific in the United States army, took the place of one.

Besides his regular staff, Johnston created a personal staff that included the Confederate governor of Kentucky and the refugee Confederate governor of Missouri. This group also included an executive of the Memphis and Charleston Railroad, a major line that ran laterally through his department. The presence of these officials in his headquarters indicated Johnston's appreciation of the political and logistical factors in warfare. Confederate Governor Thomas C. Reynolds of Missouri wrote later, "This [appointment of political figures] was one of the many incidents which showed me that he was a complete general, for, while no true soldier will permit any merely political influences around him, yet an able commander should always take into consideration, and be minutely and accurately informed of, the condition, resources, etc., of the country in which he operates."

Johnston was unable to strengthen his army enough to keep step with the Union forces opposing him. His appeals to Confederate authorities and to state governors brought only a trickle of troops. By the opening of the new year he faced a Union army that was almost twice the size of his own, and his opponents were aware that he lacked the strength to threaten them seriously. In January 1862 he wrote in disappointment to the Confederate secretary of war: "I have hoped to be able to raise an adequate force by the aid of the Governors of the several states of this department; but, notwithstanding zealous efforts on their part, thus far I have been able to draw to this

## ULYSSES S. GRANT

Born Ohio 1822; graduated U.S. Military Academy 1843, twenty-first in his class; brevetted 2d lieutenant in 4th Infantry 1843; 2d lieutenant 1845; 1st lieutenant 1847; regimental quartermaster 1847 to 1853; brevetted captain 1847 for gallant conduct in Mexican War; assigned in 1852 to duty in California, where he missed his wife and drank heavily; resigned from army in 1854 to avoid court martial; failed at a number of undertakings; appointed colonel 21st Illinois Infantry and then brigadier general volunteers in 1861;

major general volunteers 1862; gained national attention following victories at Fort Donelson, Shiloh, and Vicksburg; received thanks of Congress and promotion to major general U.S. Army in 1863; after victories around Chattanooga, appointed lieutenant general and commander of all U.S. forces in 1864. Accompanied Meade's Army of the Potomac on a bloody campaign of attrition through the Wilderness, Spotsylvania, Cold Harbor, siege of Petersburg, and the pursuit to Appomattox; commander of the U.S. Army 1864 to 1869; U.S. president 1869 to 1877. Visited Europe, suffered bankruptcy, and wrote his memoirs while dying of cancer; died in 1885 in New York City, where he is buried. "The art of war is simple enough," Grant once explained. "Find out where your enemy is. Get at him as soon as you can. Strike at him as hard as you can, and keep moving on." A staff officer said of Grant: "His face has three expressions: deep thought, extreme determination, and great simplicity and calmness."

place only a force which, when compared in number to the enemey, must be regarded as insufficient."

The opening moves against his Kentucky line were made at its extremities. In early November 1861 Brigadier General Ulysses S. Grant moved his command from its base at Cairo, Illinois, to attack a small outpost at Belmont, Missouri, across the Mississippi from Columbus. Polk's men drove the attackers off by ferrying reinforcements across the river. In mid-January Johnston's eastern force, now commanded by Brigadier General George B. Crittenden of Kentucky, attacked Union troops under Brigadier General George Thomas north of the Cumberland River in the Battle of Mill Springs (also called the Battle of Fishing Creek or the Battle of Logan's Cross Roads). The Confederates were defeated and driven back across the river.

The foregoing actions were preliminaries to a far more serious operation, an attack by Grant in the western sector of Johnston's Kentucky line. The attack came at the points where the Tennessee and Cumberland Rivers penetrated the Confederate line. The rivers were guarded by Fort Henry on the Tennessee and Fort Donelson on the Cumberland. Johnston had begun the construction of another fort, to be named Fort Heiman, on the opposite side of the Tennessee from Fort Henry, but the armament of Fort Heiman was never completed. Forts Henry and Donelson were located in Tennessee, a few miles below the Kentucky-Tennessee boundary, and were about equidistant from Bowling Green and Columbus. Construction of them began under the Tennessee authorities at a time when Kentucky was still in a neutral stance, and although Johnston's engineers found the works to be rather poorly located, the general decided, because of the shortage of time, to leave them where they were.

The forts were vulnerable to Union attack; as events would soon demonstrate, Johnston did not give them sufficient attention until it was too late. He allowed his preoccupation with the broader concerns of departmental command to divert his mind from the forts. On the morning of February 6, 1862 a joint force of 17,000 troops under Grant and a flotilla of seven gunboats commanded by Flag Officer Andrew H. Foote moved against Fort Henry. The gunboats alone quickly overpowered the fort's batteries, and at 2:00 p.m. the commander, Brigadier General Lloyd Tilghman, who had sent most of his troops to Fort Donelson and had remained with the gun crews, surrendered to Foote. Grant and Foote now turned their attention to Fort Donelson eleven miles to the east. Grant wired his superior, Major General Henry Halleck, in St. Louis, that he would take the position on February 8.

The loss of Fort Henry opened an irreparable breach in Johnston's defensive line. The Federals could now use the Tennessee River to transport and sustain an army far behind his forward positions. This made the establishment of a new defense line within the great curve of the river almost impossible. Two days after the capture of Fort Henry a Union flotilla reconnoitered the river as far south as Florence, Alabama.

On February 7, after learning of the fall of Fort Henry, Johnston met with his ranking subordinates to develop a strategy for dealing with the situation. In addition to General Hardee, commander of the Bowling Green force, the group included General P.G.T. Beauregard. Hero of Fort Sumter and Manassas, Beauregard had quarreled with Jefferson Davis, and he now found himself sent west to serve as Johnston's second-in-command. Some of his friends looked upon this as a form of exile. He reported to Johnston on February 4, just as the Fort Henry crisis was beginning to develop.

Beauregard was a product of the Creole aristocracy of Louisiana. Extremely bright (he graduated second in his class at West Point) and highly articulate, he was capable of generating flashes of strategic insight. But he was visionary, impetuous, and erratic. He was also proud, sensitive, and opinionated. Finally, he was suffering from some sort of throat infection when he appeared at Bowling Green. Johnston received

Beauregard cordially and revealed to him with absolute candor the details of his situation. Dismayed upon learning the true weakness of Johnston's entire army, Beauregard threatened to leave Kentucky at once, but Johnston persuaded him to remain.

The relationship between the two generals would exert a profound effect on the forthcoming campaign. Beauregard would make a genuine contribution to the Confederate effort, but he would also take certain actions that helped to defeat it. In his post-war account of the campaign he would sharply distort his own role in it and his overall relationship with Johnston. In effect, he would claim that all of Johnston's wise moves were made at his (Beauregard's) suggestion and all of Johnston's unwise moves over his objection. Years after the war this led to a prolonged and bitter controversy between Beauregard, supported by his partisans, and William Preston Johnston and his supporters. (The controversy still reverberates among Civil War historians.)

The meeting on February 7 occurred at the Covington House, Beauregard's Bowling Green headquarters. From this meeting came a plan of momentous importance both for the western army and for the entire Confederacy. Johnston proposed to abandon his advanced line and withdraw all his forces to undetermined locations below the Tennessee River. The two wings of the army were temporarily to act as independent forces, eventually to be united at some point below the Tennessee. Polk's wing, with Beauregard in top command, was to withdraw to Grand Junction, Tennessee (a rail junction of the Tennessee and Ohio Railroad with the Memphis and Charleston), in order to be in position to defend Memphis.

The Mississippi River was to be defended by a small fleet of Confederate gunboats under Commander George N. Hollins, first at Columbus, then in succession at Island No. 10, Fort Pillow some forty-nine miles above Memphis, and finally at Memphis. If Memphis proved to be untenable, Beauregard was to fall back to Grenada, Mississippi, and, in an extremity, to Jackson. Hardee's wing of the army plus Crittenden's troops from eastern Kentucky, with Johnston in top command, were to retire to Nashville and then to Stevenson, Alabama (on the Memphis and Charleston Railroad), and thence "according to circumstance."

Though all three generals at the meeting agreed on

## PIERRE GUSTAVE TOUTANT BEAUREGARD

Born Louisiana 1818; graduated from the U.S. Military Academy second in his 1838 class of forty-five; long an admirer of Napoleon, 2d Lieutenant Beauregard followed his hero's path by entering the artillery, but soon transferred to engineers; promoted to 1st lieutenant in 1839, he served on General Winfield Scott's staff during the Mexican War, receiving two brevets; promoted to captain in 1853, he performed engineering duties mostly in the New Orleans area until January 1861, when despite his support for secession he was appointed superintendent at West Point only to be relieved days later; he resigned his commission in February and entered Confederate service as a brigadier general; assigned to command at Charleston, South Carolina, he became an instant hero when in April he directed the reduction of Fort Sumter; ordered to Virginia, he served under General J.E. Johnston in the First Battle of Manassas, during which he exercised tactical command; in August 1861 he was elevated to full general, ranking fifth behind Samuel Cooper, A.S. Johnston, R.E. Lee, and J.E. Johnston, but his heated criticism of the government's handling of the war led to a bitter relationship with President Jefferson Davis; as a result of this rift, Beauregard was ordered west to serve under Albert Sidney Johnston; he helped orchestrate the Confederate withdrawal from Tennessee and the concentration of forces at Corinth, Mississippi; credited with organizing the army and planning the April 1862

Johnston's plan of operations, and signed a memorandum to this effect, Beauregard years later would claim to have urged a different plan, one in which the Bowling Green troops were to be transported to Fort Donelson to engage Grant there in a decisive battle. (Beauregard's claim is not supported by any contemporary evidence.) He personally wrote the memorandum, which was actually the equivalent of a set of minutes

Battle of Shiloh, he took command after Johnston was killed in action, but was forced to retreat the following day; after yielding Corinth, Beauregard took unauthorized sick leave and was replaced by General Braxton Bragg, which deepened his animosity toward Davis; returned to South Carolina, Beauregard performed admirably in thwarting several Federal attempts to seize Charleston; transferred in April 1864 to command the Department of North Carolina and Southern Virginia, he showed great skill in covering Lee's rear, when his outnumbered force halted Federal advances in the Bermuda Hundred and at Petersburg, buying valuable time for Lee's army; he still hoped for a major field command, but his relationship with Davis precluded such; instead he assumed command of the Military Division of the West, a largely administrative position with overall responsibility for Confederate forces between the Appalachian Mountains and the Mississippi River, but could do little to aid General J.B. Hood's disastrous Tennessee Campaign or oppose General W.T. Sherman's March to the Sea; Beauregard ended the war serving under J.E. Johnston in the Carolinas, surrendering with the Army of Tennessee in April 1865. Unlike many former Confederates, Beauregard prospered after the war, becoming a railroad executive and profiting from his involvement in the Louisiana Lottery; he also served as commissioner of public works in New Orleans and adjutant general of Louisiana; he died at New Orleans in 1893. General Beauregard possessed undeniable talents and was capable of outstanding generalship, but vanity, jealousy, and a penchant for developing grand strategic designs that were beyond the Confederacy's means hampered his effectiveness; his inability to work with Richmond authorities (for which Davis was as much at fault) robbed the Confederacy of a potentially valuable resource.

from the meeting. Johnston promptly wrote to Davis, setting forth the details of the decision and stating that the three generals were unanimous in reaching it. Within a few days Hardee wrote a private letter to a lady friend, remarking that all had agreed on the necessity of abandoning the Kentucky line. He said nothing of any discussion of an alternative to this plan.

Delayed by flood waters surrounding Fort Henry, Grant did not advance against Fort Donelson until the morning of February 12. The following day he invested the works with a force of 15,000 men. Meanwhile, Flag Officer Foote steamed his flotilla into position to attack the fort directly. He opened fire at mid-afternoon of the fourteenth. But the fort was well located on high ground, and its guns decisively repelled the attack. Grant settled down to a siege.

## WILLIAM PRESTON JOHNSTON

Born Kentucky 1831; the eldest son of future Confederate General Albert Sidney Johnston, William Preston Johnston was raised by maternal relatives (including his uncle, future Confederate General William Preston) following the death of his mother and his father's departure to Texas; after studying at Centre College in Danville, Kentucky, and the Western Military Institute in Georgetown, Kentucky, Johnston entered Yale University, graduating in 1852; he then studied law at the University of Louisville and soon opened a practice; with the outbreak of the Civil War, he entered Confederate service as a major in the 2d Kentucky Infantry but became lieutenant colonel of the 1st Kentucky in July 1861; he saw limited action before poor health, which plagued him throughout his life, compelled him to take leave; he returned to duty as colonel and aide-de-camp to President Jefferson Davis; in this capacity he

The fort's garrison now equaled or exceeded Grant's invest-ing force. Johnston, after deciding the position could not be held, had made the serious mistake of ordering an additional several thousand troops into it. He instructed the commanding officer, Brigadier General John Floyd, to break out and join the main body of Johnston's withdrawing army at Nashville if Fort Donelson could not be held. Early on the fifteenth the Confederates made an attack on a portion of Grant's line and temporarily opened the road to Nashville. Then, unaccount-ably, they returned to their original defensive positions. That evening General Floyd and the next ranking Confederate, Brigadier General Gideon Pillow, wired Johnston that they had achieved "victory complete and glorious."

Nothing could have been further from the truth. After the

conducted numerous inspection tours and served as a liaison between Davis and his generals; he fueled controversy when he reported that his father was on the verge of a great victory in the Battle of Shiloh at the time of his death, and that General P.G.T. Beauregard failed to seize the opportunity presented; during the closing stages of the war Johnston saw action around Richmond and joined Davis and other members of the staff in flight as the Confederacy collapsed; captured with Davis in Georgia, he was imprisoned for many weeks at Fort Delaware; on his release, he lived briefly in Canada before returning to Louisville and the practice of law; in 1867 he accepted from Robert E. Lee a faculty position at Washington College (Washington and Lee University) in Lexington, Virginia; in 1880 he became president of Louisiana State University, and in 1884 was instrumental in founding Tulane University, serving as its president until his death in 1899. Always given to intellectual pursuits, Johnston wrote extensively on topics ranging from English litera-ture to family history, including several volumes of poetry; his most popular work, a biography of his father, *The Life of Gen. Albert Sidney Johnston*, pub-lished in 1878, further stirred the Shiloh controversy—a contentious war of words with Beauregard over his father's generalship.

Southern soldiers returned to the Fort Donelson lines, Grant quickly closed the ring on them. During the night the Confederate generals decided that their plight was hopeless and surrender inevitable. Floyd and Pillow passed the command to the hapless third in command, General Buckner. Floyd and his Virginia regiments left for Nashville by steamboat. Pillow and his staff crossed the Tennessee in a small boat and escaped. At dawn Buckner capitulated to his old friend and West Point classmate Grant on terms of "unconditional surrender." Only the unknown cavalry leader, Lieutenant Colonel Nathan Bedford Forrest, got out with a portion of his command.

The loss of Fort Donelson and its troops, along with the loss of Fort Henry, placed Johnston's entire army in the direst peril. One fourth of the army east of the Mississippi was gone, captured at Fort Donelson. The two wings were separated by almost two hundred miles, with a strong Union force between them on the Tennessee and Cumberland Rivers, and an even stronger Union army now commanded by Major General Don Carlos Buell marching upon Nashville from Kentucky.

Were these losses unavoidable? Ought Johnston have done what Beauregard later claimed to have urged him to do: rush to Fort Donelson with his Bowling Green force in an effort to defeat Grant there? Such an operation might have been successful, but any conclusion drawn on the matter would be purely speculative. There were serious obstacles to such a course. Johnston reasoned that the risk of being crushed between the armies of Grant and Buell was too great for him to accept.

Grant wrote years after the war that Johnston should have taken the risk; that the result would not have been worse if Johnston and his entire army had been captured at Fort Donelson. Perhaps Grant was right in saying Johnston should have taken the risk, but Grant was demonstrably wrong in saying that the loss of the fort and a part of his Bowling Green force was as bad as the loss of Johnston and his entire wing of the army would have been. Grant ignored the role played later by Johnston and his troops in checking the Union advance in the Mississippi Valley.

Notwithstanding what Johnston could or should have done, his decisions and actions resulted in the loss of the state of Kentucky and the western half of Tennessee, including the important city of Nashville. Quite possibly he lacked the resources in men, arms, and transportation to have held the area. But if it could not have been held, then he ought to have saved all of his army. Instead, he lost both the area and a significant portion of his troops. His generalship fell short of the demands of this critical campaign.

# 2
# RETREAT AND CONCENTRATION

The surrender of Fort Donelson opened the Cumberland River to Union forces and threatened Johnston's entire Bowling Green column with immediate capture. The Confederates were encamped in the village of Edgefield on the north bank of the river opposite Nashville the night of February 15 when Johnston received the thrilling victory message foolishly sent by General Floyd. Johnston was stunned when later that night he learned that the fort was to be surrendered at dawn. Exclaiming, "I must save this army," he immediately began to move his troops across the river into Nashville.

The city's population greeted him joyously, because the morning newspapers announced a Confederate victory at Fort Donelson. When the truth became known, the popular celebration gave way to rage and panic. Rioting broke out in the streets, and a mob stormed Johnston's headquarters. A prominent citizen wired Davis, beseeching him to come to Tennessee in order to save the state. Others begged Davis to take personal command of the western army, or to appoint Beauregard, Major General Braxton Bragg, or Major General John C. Breckinridge (former vice president of the United States) to the position. The Tennessee state legislature sent a delegation to demand Johnston's dismissal, saying, "He is no general." But Jefferson Davis rebuffed the delegates with the declaration that if Johnston was not a general, the Confederacy had no general and had better quit the war.

While Johnston was involved in the disastrous Fort Donelson affair and the evacuation of Nashville, Beauregard set about to carry out the provisions of the Covington House conference of February 7 as they applied to the western wing of the army, mainly the troops of General Polk at Columbus. Because the decision was already made that Columbus and Fort Donelson could not be held, Beauregard wrote Johnston on February 12, urging the immediate withdrawal of the troops from Columbus in order to redeploy them for the defense of the portion of Tennessee lying west of the Tennessee River.

Two days later Johnston met with Beauregard in Nashville to give him an answer to his recommendation and to discuss the overall departmental strategic and operational situation. Unfortunately for a complete understanding of the events that were about to occur, no contemporary record of this meeting survived. Years after the war Beauregard claimed that Johnston approved the withdrawal of the Columbus troops but told Beauregard that he would need also the approval of the Confederate War Department before taking the step. According to Beauregard's account, the rest of their conversation merely repeated the decisions already announced in the Covington House conference. That evening Beauregard left for the western region of the department.

Establishing his headquarters at Jackson in western Tennessee, located on the Mobile and Ohio Railroad fifty miles north of the Mississippi line, Beauregard obtained War

Department approval to withdraw the Columbus troops and deploy them in towns along the railroad. He also set about energetically to repeat the requests previously made by Johnston for reinforcements.

Alarmed by the calamity that had occurred in the western department, Richmond authorities now ordered a remarkable massing of forces there. As early as February 10, in response

## BRAXTON BRAGG

Born North Carolina 1817; graduated U.S. Military Academy fifth in the 1837 class of fifty; appointed 2d lieutenant 3rd Artillery; promoted to 1st lieutenant in 1838 and to captain in 1846; participated in the Seminole War and won three brevet promotions for gallant conduct during the Mexican War; in 1849 married Eliza Brooks Ellis, daughter of a Louisiana sugar cane planter; after routine garrison duty on the frontier, he resigned his brevet lieutenant colonelcy in 1856 to become a Louisiana sugar planter; in 1861 appointed Confederate brigadier general and assigned to Pensacola, Florida, where he changed the volunteers he found there into drilled and disciplined soldiers; promoted to major general and assigned command of the Gulf Coast from Pensacola to Mobile; in 1862 he received orders to move his troops by rail to join General A. S. Johnston's army at Corinth, Mississippi, for the Battle of Shiloh, during which Bragg served as army chief of staff and commanded a corps; after Johnston's death, upon the recommendation of his successor, General P.G.T. Beauregard, Bragg was promoted to full general; in June he in turn replaced General Beauregard when that officer took an unauthorized sick leave; deciding to invade Kentucky, Bragg moved the bulk of his army from Tupelo, Mississippi, to Chattanooga, Tennessee, by rail, and then

to Johnston's urgent request, Brigadier General Daniel Ruggles was on his way with four regiments from New Orleans. Johnston ordered him to report to Beauregard. Three regiments of reinforcements sent to Chattanooga by the War Department were forwarded by Johnston to Beauregard. General Braxton Bragg wrote from Mobile to the secretary of war, saying, "Should we not give up the seaboard now and con-

joined General E. Kirby Smith in a bold invasion of Kentucky; checked at Perryville in October by General D.C. Buell, Bragg retreated to Murfreesboro, Tennessee, where he fought a bloody battle against General W.S. Rosecrans in late 1862 and early 1863; Rosecrans's Tullahoma Campaign in June 1863 compelled Bragg to abandon Tennessee, but after receiving General James Longstreet's Corps from Virginia in September as reinforcements for the Battle of Chickamauga, he drove the Federals back into Chattanooga and began a siege that lasted until General U.S. Grant arrived from Mississippi in November 1863 and drove the Confederates back into Georgia; relieved of command of the Army of Tennessee, Bragg became President Davis's military adviser in February 1864; he exercised considerable power and served the president and the Confederacy well during the eight months he held this position, but his appointment came too late in the war for him to have a determinative impact; in January 1865, while still serving as the president's military adviser, Bragg engaged in his most ineffective performance as a field commander:  he failed to prevent the Federals from taking Fort Fisher, which protected Wilmington, North Carolina, the last Confederate port open to blockade runners; Bragg spent the last weeks of the war under the command of General J.E. Johnston attempting to check General W.T. Sherman's advance; Bragg and his wife were part of the Confederate flight from Richmond until their capture in Georgia; Bragg, who lived in relative poverty after the war, died in Galveston, Texas, in 1876, and is buried in Mobile. Never a great field commander, he had talents the Confederacy needed but seldom used:  the army possessed no better disciplinarian or drillmaster; an able organizer and administrator, he excelled as an inspector, possessed a good eye for strategy, and proved himself a dedicated patriot.

centrate all our means on the vital point?" When a Beauregard staff officer reached Bragg to request him to unite with Beauregard, he found that Bragg and his ten thousand well-drilled soldiers had already been ordered north and were preparing to leave the following day for the town of Corinth in northeastern Mississippi. Fresh levies of troops were raised by the western Confederate states to strengthen their hard-pressed army.

On the day of the surrender of Fort Donelson Johnston left Nashville with the eastern wing of the army and marched his column to Murfreesboro, some thirty-five miles to the south-east. The march was made with extreme difficulty, for the troops were demoralized over the abandonment of Kentucky and Nashville. Some of them clamored to remain and fight; some wept in their anger and frustration; some said that Nashville ought to be burned down in order to keep it out of enemy possession. Johnston wrote Davis, "Some of the troops were disheartened." In truth, all of them were.

Even General Hardee and Colonel Mackall had lost faith in Johnston's leadership. Hardee wrote his friend that the "precipitate" retreat from Nashville was the cause of much demoralization in the ranks. "In my judgment," he said, "nothing can save us except the presence of the President, who ought to come here, assume command, and call on the people to rally to his standard."

In spite of the demoralization, Johnston held to his purpose and kept his column intact and moving. At Murfreesboro he waited for Crittenden's small force from eastern Kentucky and for the rear guard from Nashville. When these troops arrived he added them to those he had brought from Bowling Green and formed the entire force into a small, compact army of approximately twenty thousand. He organized them into three divisions with Hardee, Crittenden, and Pillow each command-ing a division. The Texas Rangers and Forrest's cavalry he kept under his immediate command.

Johnston now faced the crucial decision of where to go from Murfreesboro, and how to get there. His ultimate objective, as set forth in the Covington House conference, was to unite the two wings of his army in order to develop the strength to oppose the Federals effectively. The closest and most convenient line of operations for this purpose lay along the Memphis and Charleston Railroad, which ran east-west below the great crescent of the Tennessee River. Theoretically, the town of Corinth, Mississippi, was the ideal place for this concentration, and eventually it would occur there. The community was located at the intersection of the Memphis and

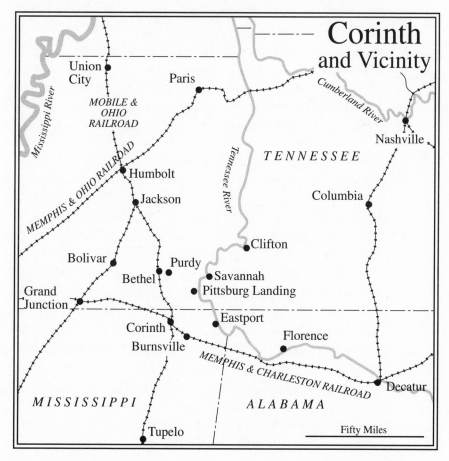

Charleston Railroad with the Mobile and Ohio Railroad, which ran north-south from Columbus, Kentucky, to Mobile.

Even before the fall of Fort Donelson Brigadier General Leroy Pope Walker, commander of Alabama state forces, had written to Johnston emphasizing the serious consequences of losing the fort because of the effect it would have in exposing Corinth. From Florence, Alabama, Walker wrote: "It is not only the Tennessee River up to this point which is threatened, but also the Memphis and Charleston Road at Corinth, Miss. These roads constitute the vertebrae of the Confederacy. . . . A large proportion of the population of the counties of Hardin and Wayne [Tennessee] is in sympathy with the enemy, and either Savannah or Hamburg, in Tennessee, or Eastport, in Mississippi, will be made the base of his operations."

But Corinth was dangerously close to the Tennessee River (22 miles), and thus subject to seizure by the Federals before the Confederates could unite there. Apparently for this reason neither Johnston nor Beauregard at first considered it a feasible place for their concentration. The town was not mentioned in the Covington House memorandum or in the correspondence or conversation of either general during the early stage of the movement. Soon, however, encouraged by the delay in the Federal advance up the Tennessee, the Confederate generals began to think about Corinth.

Not until March 13 did Union Brigadier General Charles F. Smith debark a force at Savannah, Tennessee; three days later he established his camp at Pittsburg Landing on the west bank of the river nine miles above Savannah. Shortly Grant arrived and took command of this army of five divisions (approximately 35,000 troops). An additional division joined them later. Grant made his headquarters in Savannah. Meanwhile, General Halleck, Union commander in the West, from his headquarters in St. Louis ordered Buell to march his army from Nashville to Pittsburg Landing. Grant was to await Buell's arrival before proceeding against Corinth.

Beauregard could get his wing of the Confederate army to Corinth with relative ease and comparatively little risk. His troops were outside of the arc of the Tennessee River and could be hauled on the Mobile and Ohio Railroad to their destination.

The difficulties and dangers for Johnston's wing were far greater. Much of his route to Corinth lay within the arc of the river. By prompt action with their gunboats and transports the Federals could intercept his march and trap his force between their army on the river and Buell's army from Nashville. On February 22 Major Jeremy Gilmer, Johnston's chief of engineers, wrote his wife from Murfreesboro, saying that the army would move from there to Decatur, Alabama, or to Chattanooga, or to some other point south. Clearly, and wisely, Johnston was keeping his options open in order to avoid the trap.

After the Civil War Beauregard and William Preston Johnston argued vehemently about who actually selected Corinth as the junction place. Beauregard said he made the choice and sent Governor Isham Harris as an emissary to Murfreesboro to persuade a bewildered and indecisive Johnston to come to Corinth.

The Creole general's claim differed from contemporary accounts. The earliest documentary hint that Johnston might be headed for Corinth appeared in Major Gilmer's statement that listed Decatur as a possible objective in the Confederate march; this town lay on the Memphis and Charleston Railroad and on the best route to Corinth. Five days later Johnston wrote the Confederate secretary of war, stating positively that he was headed for Decatur in order to cooperate or unite with Beauregard. Governor Harris later explained that when he arrived at Murfreesboro he found Johnston already preparing to take his force to Corinth. Apparently, both generals independently chose Corinth, then reached an agreement when Harris talked with Johnston.

Beauregard was understandably anxious that Johnston make the move with the utmost dispatch. On March 2 he wrote Johnston that the great battle of the war would soon be fought at or near Corinth and urged him to bring his troops there by rail; Beauregard followed this with one telegram or letter after another, repeating his recommendations for speeding up the movement.

Johnston was aware of the need for haste, but circumstances dictated a deliberate march. He appreciated fully the advantage of moving by rail instead of by foot, but he lacked the facilities to move everything by rail. Gilmer explained later: "It was simply impossible [to ship the troops by train] without sacrificing the supplies and munitions on which the subsistence and armament of the command depended. The

## ISHAM G. HARRIS

Born Tennessee 1818; a self-taught lawyer and successful businessman, Harris became a leading Democrat in his native state; elected to the state senate in 1847, he was a forceful advocate of slavery; cast out of office in 1851, he established a successful legal practice in Memphis, and in 1855 was appointed to the state supreme court; returning to politics, in 1857 he was elected governor of Tennessee; reelected overwhelmingly in 1859, he campaigned for Southern Democrat John C. Breckinridge in the 1860 presidential election; but with Abraham Lincoln's victory and the subsequent secession of the Deep South, Harris was left in a precarious position; his first call for Tennessee's secession failed, but he continued to support the Southern position, rejecting Lincoln's call for volunteers following the attack on Fort Sumter in April 1861; he then initiated a de facto relationship with the Confederate government, even before he managed to arrange a

entire transportation capacity of the railroads was taxed to the utmost, and even then immense quantities of meat and other commissary supplies were left at [points along the way]."

Johnston marched his force by foot from Murfreesboro to Shelbyville to Fayetteville, Tennessee, and thence to Huntsville and Decatur, Alabama. He made the move with an uneasy eye on his enemy. "The General wears a very anxious face," wrote Gilmer early in the march. "Still he expresses confidence that better fortune awaits us." Not until the Federals pitched camp near Pittsburg Landing could Johnston be reasonably sure that they would fail to intercept his march, and he kept his mind open as to the course he would follow if they should do so.

He was also concerned that the Federals might launch an immediate movement against Memphis from their base at

successful referendum on secession; quickly, Harris raised 100,000 volunteers for military service, but preparations for the defense of Tennessee proved inadequate; the violation of Kentucky's neutrality opened Tennessee to invasion from the north—something Harris had considered unlikely; in February 1862 the surrenders of Forts Henry and Donelson initiated the collapse of the Tennessee line, and the Confederate forces of General Albert Sidney Johnston were forced to retreat into Mississippi; when Nashville fell to Union forces, Harris fled to Memphis, but with a new Unionist government in place, he was left powerless; although he retained his title, Harris now joined the military staff of General Johnston, and was present at his death during the Battle of Shiloh; thereafter he worked as a volunteer on the staffs of every commander of what became the Army of Tennessee; rendering valuable service to Generals Braxton Bragg, Joseph Johnston, and John Bell Hood, he was present during almost every battle fought by the Army of Tennessee; with the collapse of the Confederacy, Harris became a fugitive; charged by Tennessee authorities with treason, he fled to Mexico and then England, but after two years he was allowed to return; he resumed his law practice, and in 1877 he was elected to the U.S. Senate, in which he served until his death at Washington in 1897.

Pittsburg Landing. Upon receiving word from General Bragg that they had begun a march in that direction, Johnston suggested by wire from Decatur that Beauregard consider taking a position behind the Hatchie River near Bolivar in western Tennessee. Bragg's information turned out to be erroneous, and Johnston did not return to the subject.

Johnston has been criticized for remaining with the eastern wing of the army. He should have gone to Corinth, some students of the war believe, in order personally to coordinate the concentration of troops. There is justice in this criticism, if it be assumed that someone else, presumably Hardee, could have brought the eastern column to Corinth as effectually as Johnston did. Such an assumption is dubious. All of Johnston's subordinates, including Hardee, believed the move to Corinth to be impossible. Hardee now looked to Beauregard and Bragg as the only sources of Confederate hope. Johnston was obliged to overrule his shaken underlings in order to carry out his plan for the concentration of his forces.

The movement was the more difficult because of the severe weather and widespread sickness among the soldiers. The roads turned to quagmire under the winter rains. Gilmer wrote, "We live and move in mud and water, and the roads have come to such a pass that we can't move much longer." They nevertheless continued the brutal march, transporting the sick in freight cars and hospitalizing them in improvised infirmaries and private residences along the way. Only their commander's unshakable will and faith in his own judgment kept the column moving.

Johnston knew that Buell's column by a timely and vigorous march from Nashville was capable of reaching Grant's Federal army on the Tennessee River before he could join forces with Beauregard. As early as March 11, before Buell left Nashville or the Federals settled at Pittsburg Landing, Johnston predicted a junction of the two Union commands and carried out a remarkably successful program for delaying Buell as much as possible. Johnston did this with his cavalry, sending such bold troopers as John Hunt Morgan, Forrest, J. S. Scott, Benjamin H. Helm, and Wirt Adams to harass Buell and burn the bridges across the streams in his path. Morgan was especially audacious, riding on one occasion to the edge of Nashville, driving in the Federal pickets, and observing and reporting on activities within the city.

Other actions by Johnston deceived his opponents and confused them in their views of Confederate strategy. Beauregard wrote him to suggest that he spread rumors of his intention to move to Chattanooga instead of Corinth. Actually, Johnston was already doing things that planted this belief in his enemies' minds. The initial Confederate retreat to Murfreesboro, more on the route to Chattanooga than to Corinth, tended to have this effect. Johnston ordered that all mail for his army be sent to Chattanooga and that a quartermaster depot be established there. Both Grant and Buell expressed the opinion that Johnston was headed for this city. On March 7 a Confederate spy reported to General Bragg in Corinth that the Federal leaders were convinced that Chattanooga was Johnston's destination. By then his column was several days on the march to Corinth.

From Decatur Johnston replied to a letter from Davis that requested details of the loss of Fort Henry and Fort Donelson. Johnston indicated that he lacked the strength to hold these positions and that his troop losses there resulted from the mistakes of his subordinates. He was generous, however, to Floyd and Pillow, saying that though they might have been able to extricate the troops, "justice requires to look at events as they appeared at the time and not alone by the light of subsequent information."

Nor did Johnston complain about the public condemnation brought upon him by the loss of the forts. Admitting that the defeat had been disastrous, he said that he had observed silence because he believed it to be in the best interest of the cause. He explained: "I refrained [from speaking out] well knowing that heavy censures would fall upon me, but convinced that it was better to endure them for the present and defer to a more propitious time an investigation [of the conduct of Floyd and Pillow]. . . . The test of merit in my profession with the people is success; it is a hard rule but I think it right."

Johnston's various measures enabled him to carry out successfully his plan of concentrating the wings of his army. He crossed his troops over the Tennessee River on the Memphis and Charleston Railroad bridge at Decatur, from which point

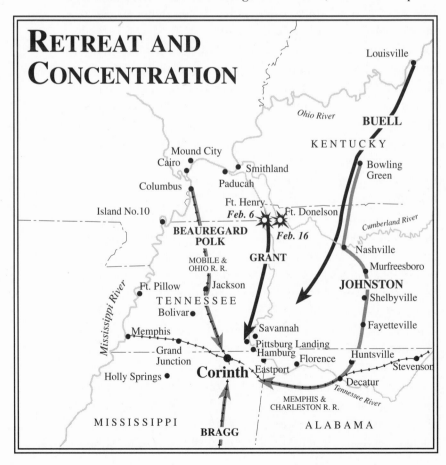

he shuttled them and their arms and equipment by rail to Corinth. He was able to do so by securing for his purpose a supply of locomotives and cars of the Western and Atlantic Railroad south of Chattanooga. He arrived in Corinth on March 23, followed within two or three days by the remainder of his column.

Although he succeeded in joining the two wings of his army east of the Mississippi, he failed in his efforts to strengthen his total force by bringing troops from west of the river. Beauregard attempted as early as February 21 to persuade General Van Dorn to bring his army of approximately 20,000 from Arkansas to join the force that was being collected in western Tennessee.

With a breathtakingly broad interpretation of Johnston's statement that he was to act independently, Beauregard wrote Van Dorn that together they could launch a great counteroffensive that would regain Kentucky, take Cairo, Illinois, and possibly capture St. Louis. He made no mention of Johnston or his wing of the army in elaborating this ambitious scheme. "What say you to this brilliant programme," Beauregard queried Van Dorn, "which I know is fully practicable if we can get the forces?"

Van Dorn was not persuaded. He had a plan for defeating Major General Samuel R. Curtis's Union army in Arkansas, then moving to threaten or seize St. Louis. He believed this would not only protect Arkansas from the Federals but would at the same time constitute an important diversion in favor of Johnston's efforts east of the river. On February 24 he wrote Johnston that he was about to launch his attack. Johnston either did not reply, or his reply was lost. On March 6 Van Dorn attacked Curtis in the Battle of Pea Ridge (or Elkhorn Tavern) and was defeated.

A victory by Van Dorn would indeed have diverted a significant body of Union troops from western Tennessee for the protection of St. Louis. General Halleck recorded that he had intended to employ for this purpose some of the force that went instead to Grant. But Johnston ought shortly after the Battle of Pea Ridge to have ordered Van Dorn east of the Mississippi. He failed to do so. Beauregard wrote Van Dorn again on March 19, renewing his call upon him, but Van Dorn paid him no heed. Not until Johnston arrived at Corinth and discussed the situation with Beauregard and Bragg did he order the Arkansas commander to bring his army to Corinth. This turned out to be too late. Inadequate transportation and the flooding of Arkansas rivers delayed his arrival until after the critical battle had been fought.

When Johnston reached Corinth he freely expressed his gratitude to Beauregard and Bragg for what they had already done to concentrate a striking force there. He said to Bragg, "Your prompt and decisive move, Sir, has saved me, and saved the country." He offered the field command of the army to Beauregard, saying that he would move his departmental head-quarters to Memphis or Holly Springs, Mississippi. This was an extraordinary overture, but not an unheard-of one. Perhaps, as Johnston's son later explained it, Johnston was simply mak-ing a courteous gesture to emphasize the sincerity of his grati-tude to Beauregard. A brief time earlier the Creole general had made a similar offer, to serve under Bragg (his inferior in rank and prestige), in requesting that Bragg's army be brought to Corinth.

Johnston's closest friends besought him not to offer the command to Beauregard. [Confederate] Governor George W. Johnson of Kentucky, who was with the army, wrote him to say, "You must not do this. I beg that you will not do it, both for your own fame and the good of the country. If I hear that you are resolved on this course, I will despair of our cause. It will sink under the curse of Heaven, upon a people, who joined like wolves . . . to hunt down the noblest and purest man it has been my good-fortune to know." Johnston did, however, make the offer. Beauregard chivalrously declined it, whereupon

## LEONIDAS POLK

Born North Carolina 1806; attended the University of North Carolina and then the U.S. Military Academy, graduating eighth in his class of thirty-eight in 1827; brevetted 2d lieutenant and posted to artillery, Polk served only a few months before resigning to study for the Episcopal ministry; ordained a deacon in 1830, he became Missionary Bishop of the Southwest in 1838 and Bishop of Louisiana in 1841; assisted in the establishment of the University of the South at Sewanee, Tennessee; at the outbreak of the Civil War, Polk accepted a major general's commission from his close friend Confederate President Jefferson Davis; Polk's departmental command consisted of parts of Arkansas and western Tennessee. In September 1861 he violated Kentucky's professed neutrality by occupying Columbus, opening that state to Federal invasion; commanded a corps with gallantry but little skill at Shiloh and in the invasion of Kentucky; promoted to lieutenant general in October 1862, he directed a corps at Murfreesboro and a wing at Chickamauga; his overt criticism of General Braxton Bragg resulted in his banishment from the Army of Tennessee; he was given command of the Department of Alabama, Mississippi, and East Louisiana where he remained until ordered, in May 1864, to join the Army of Tennessee, now headed by Bragg's replacement General J.E. Johnston; Polk led his army (in effect, a corps) during the opening stages of the Atlanta Campaign; on June 14, 1864 he was instantly killed when struck by a solid shot while surveying Federal positions from Pine Mountain near Marietta, Georgia. General Polk's impact on the Confederate cause was largely negative. His violation of Kentucky neutrality proved irreparable and his feud with Bragg severely damaged the effectiveness of the Army of Tennessee. Davis's reluctance to remove Polk only exacerbated the situation.

Johnston took over the command of the entire combined force and named the Louisianan second-in-command.

Johnston now had an army of approximately 40,000 effective troops concentrated at a point within one day's march of the enemy. He and his associates, with a total force in the department of only approximately half the numbers of their opponents, had, through superior strategic vision, operational proficiency, daring, and force of will, assembled an army approximately equal to the one that directly confronted them, thus creating for themselves a remarkable opportunity for a decisive victory. But the Confederates, brought together in haste and confusion, were woefully disorganized, untrained,

## WILLIAM J. HARDEE

Born Georgia 1815; Hardee was graduated from the U.S. Military Academy in 1838, twenty-sixth in his class of forty-five; commissioned into the 2d Dragoons, he served in Florida and was promoted to 1st lieutenant in 1839; he studied at the Royal Cavalry School at Saumur, France, returning to the U.S. in 1842; promoted to captain in 1844, he was captured early in the Mexican War but returned to duty and earned two brevets; afterward, he taught cavalry tactics at West Point and served on the frontier; his *Rifle and Light Infantry Tactics*, published in 1855, became the Army's standard training manual for years to come; also that year he was promoted to major in the newly formed 2d Cavalry Regiment, an elite unit that included Albert Sidney Johnston, Robert E. Lee, George Thomas, E. Kirby Smith, Earl Van Dorn, and John B. Hood among several other future Civil War generals; after service in Texas, Hardee became commandant of cadets at West

and poorly armed. Many of the troops, including their officers, were entirely without military experience. Johnston set about at once with what General Bragg described as "cool, quiet self-control" to forge the conglomeration of raw soldiers into an army. He would have a brief two weeks in which to accomplish this miracle.

Wisely, he delegated major tasks to his ranking subordinates, Beauregard and Bragg. He ordered Beauregard to draw up a plan of organization. The Louisianan submitted a plan in which the force was designated the Army of the Mississippi and divided into three corps: the First Corps, consisting of 9,136 troops, was commanded by Polk; the Second Corps, with

Point; he was promoted to lieutenant colonel in 1860, but resigned in January 1861 after Georgia's secession from the Union; he soon entered Confederate service as a colonel and was elevated to brigadier general in June 1861; after organizing troops in Arkansas, he led them to Kentucky; promoted to major general in October 1861, he commanded a corps at Shiloh the following April; thereafter most of his service was with the Army of Tennessee; promoted to lieutenant general in October 1862, he led his corps with great skill at Perryville, Murfreesboro, and Chattanooga, where his stand at Missionary Ridge helped save the army from total destruction; following General Braxton Bragg's removal in December 1863, Hardee temporarily headed the army but declined the permanent command; during the 1864 Atlanta Campaign, he openly resented Hood's promotion to command the Army, and performed inconsistently; after Atlanta's fall he was reassigned at his own request and commanded troops in opposition to General W.T. Sherman's March to the Sea and in the Carolinas; he surrendered with General J.E. Johnston in April 1865; after the war he settled at Selma, Alabama, where he engaged in planting and various other enterprises; he died at Wytheville, Virginia, in 1873. Known as "Old Reliable," General Hardee was among the Confederacy's most experienced and competent corps commanders; his inability to get along with Bragg and Hood, however, proved quite detrimental.

13,598 soldiers, was headed by Bragg; and the Third Corps, 6,789 strong, was led by Hardee. Three reserve brigades, comprising a total of 6,439 troops, were commanded by Crittenden, who shortly was replaced by Brigadier General John C. Breckinridge. The reserve was stationed at Burnsville, Mississippi, fifteen miles east of Corinth on the Memphis and Charleston Railroad. The bulk of the cavalry and artillery were unassigned and left under the direct control of the commanding general.

This represented an exceptionally rational organization. Compact and simple, it provided a clear and efficient chain of command through the three corps leaders, with an infantry reserve and the cavalry and artillery to be employed at the commander's discretion. Beauregard later took all the credit for devising the plan. He claimed that Johnston accepted it without making a change in it. This was perhaps true, but Beauregard revealed that Johnston discussed with him the general principles of the plan before it was formally drawn up and submitted. Also, the details bore a marked similarity to those of Johnston's plan for the organization of his wing of the army while it was in Murfreesboro. Johnston may well have contributed significantly to the plan for the organization of the force at Corinth.

Johnston appointed Bragg to the temporary position of chief of staff in addition to his duties as a corps commander. As chief of staff he bore the direct responsibility for the training, discipline, and supply of the army. This assignment suited Bragg perfectly. Throughout his career he had been known as a trainer and disciplinarian of exceptional capabilities.

Bragg's vaunted talents would be tested to their limits. He later described without exaggeration the problems he faced. "It was a heterogeneous mass," he wrote, "in which there was more enthusiasm than discipline, more capacity than knowledge, and more valor than instruction. . . . The task of organizing such a command in four weeks [it actually turned out to be only half this long a period] and supplying it. . . was simply appalling."

He found the troops in possession of a bewildering variety of arms and equipment. He said, "Rifles—rifled and smooth bore muskets, some of them originally percussion, others hastily altered from flint locks by Yankee contractors, many still with the old flint and steel and shotguns of all sizes and patterns held place in the same regiments." He went about the task with admirable will and vigor and in an incredibly short period of time transformed the "heterogeneous mass" into a semblance of a trained, disciplined, and equipped army.

The initial great encounter of the Civil War was about ready to occur.

# 3
## DECISION FOR BATTLE

The decision to attack Grant was the first truly bold Confederate field decision made in the war. Beauregard later implied that he first made it and persuaded Johnston to it after his arrival in Corinth. The records indicate otherwise.

Johnston's only purpose in concentrating the wings of his army was to strike a decisive blow, or blows, at the Union forces that were penetrating his department. This purpose was implicit in the Covington House decision in Bowling Green and in all of his subsequent decisions and actions. It was first revealed explicitly in a private letter from Major Gilmer to his wife shortly before the Confederates reached Decatur in their march to Corinth. In explaining that Johnston was alert to the possibility that the Federals might seize the town before the arrival of his troops, Gilmer said the commander was determined to attack Grant there if possible. If that should prove to be impossible, Gilmer explained, then Johnston would withdraw farther south and await a more favorable opportunity for an attack.

The idea of a direct counterattack strongly appealed to Johnston. Once in writing to chide his daughter for her negligence in correspondence (just when he was preparing to send his letter he received one from her) he said, "You have some of the high and rare qualities of a good General. You know when to take the initiative. You anticipated my attack by making one." At Corinth he proposed to do precisely that: anticipate a Union attack by launching his own.

A few days after joining forces with Beauregard he received advice from both Jefferson Davis and Robert E. Lee, discreetly urging him to attack Grant's army. Lee wrote, "I need not tell you when your army is united, to deal a blow at the enemy in your front if possible, before his rear [Buell's army] gets up from Nashville. You have him divided now, keep him so if you can." This was eminently sound counsel, but it was unnecessary; by the time either letter reached Johnston his army was united and he was in the midst of feverish preparations to do exactly what the writers recommended.

By early April Johnston realized that time quickly was running out on him. Though his troops were still sadly wanting in training and equipment, and Van Dorn's reinforcing column was still far away, he could wait no longer. On April 1 he issued a warning order, alerting his corps commanders to be prepared for a movement to meet the Federals within twenty-four hours. The following night (about one o'clock the morning of April 3) he issued his order for the movement to begin.

Two developments caused him to do so. Shortly before ten o'clock General Polk received from Major General Benjamin Cheatham, the commander of a division posted at Bethel Station on the Mobile and Ohio Railroad approximately twenty miles north of Corinth, a message that a portion of the Union army was threatening his command. Polk forwarded the message to Beauregard, who found in it an indication that Grant's army was now divided. He sent the message to Johnston with an endorsement that said, "Now is the moment to advance, and strike the enemy at Pittsburg Landing."

At about the same time Johnston received word from Forrest that Buell's army was on its way swiftly to join Grant. Johnston now decided to make his move at once. He wired Davis: "General Buell is in motion, 30,000 strong, rapidly from Columbia [Tennessee] by Clifton to Savannah. [Brigadier General O.M.] Mitchel behind him with 10,000. Confederate forces, 40,000 ordered forward to offer battle near Pittsburg. . . . Hope engagement before Buell can form junction."

Years later Beauregard and his former chief of staff, Colonel Thomas Jordan, gave a version of the affair in which General Cheatham's message, Beauregard's endorsing state-

## Don Carlos Buell

Born Ohio 1818; raised in Indiana, Buell was graduated from the U.S. Military Academy in 1841, thirty-second in his class of fifty-two; commissioned a 2d lieutenant and posted to infantry, he served against the Seminoles in Florida; promoted to 1st lieutenant during the Mexican War, he also earned two brevets and was seriously wounded at Churubusco; after the war he held a series of staff positions until the outbreak of the Civil War; he was lieutenant colonel and adjutant general of the Department of the Pacific when appointed brigadier general of U.S. Volunteers in May 1861; he commanded a division under General George B. McClellan and helped organize the Army of the Potomac; in November 1861 he assumed command of the Army of the Ohio for a proposed strike into East Tennessee; Buell instead received reluctant authorization to move on the Tennessee capital of Nashville, which his army took with little opposition; promoted to major general

ment, and Colonel Jordan's persuasive logic became the major factors in bringing a vacillating and undecided Johnston to his decision. According to Jordan's account, supported by Beauregard, Jordan bore the message with Beauregard's notation, to Johnston, who protested that his army was not ready for battle. Jordan claimed that he was obliged to talk the reluctant commander into ordering an attack.

But Jordan's account was altogether inconsistent with Johnston's earlier order to his commanders to prepare for a move to meet the enemy, or with the reason given by Johnston for ordering the attack. Significantly, Johnston's message to Davis that announced the intended attack made no mention of a division of the Union army. Clearly, Johnston's real reason for issuing the order was the strategic one: his awareness that

U.S.V. in March 1862; moving to join General U.S. Grant's army at Pittsburg Landing, Buell's force arrived late on the first day of the Battle of Shiloh; on the second day the combined armies of Buell and Grant drove the Confederates from the field; during the campaign against Corinth, Buell led the Army of the Ohio under the overall command of General Henry Halleck; ordered in June 1862 to advance on Chattanooga, Buell was stymied by Confederate resistance; promoted to colonel in the regular establishment in July 1862; forced to withdraw into Kentucky to oppose the Confederate invasion of that state, he turned back General Braxton Bragg's army at Perryville in October, but failed to pursue aggressively the retreating Confederates; for this failure he was relieved of his command; while a military commission reviewed his performance he remained without orders for more than a year; although the commission brought no charges, Buell was mustered out of the Volunteers in May 1864; a month later he resigned his regular commission; he settled in Kentucky, where he operated an ironworks and coal mine; he died at his Kentucky home in 1898. General Buell possessed undeniable administrative talents and was capable of solid battlefield leadership; his ouster perhaps owed more to his close friendship with McClellan and the rise of Grant than to his performance.

he must strike before Buell joined Grant.

Johnston then did something that would turn out to cripple seriously his effort in the coming enterprise. He delegated to Beauregard the task of preparing the advance and attack order.

Two generally parallel roads led from Corinth toward Pittsburg Landing: the Ridge Road (apparently the better of the two) and the Monterey Road, so named because it ran through the village of Monterey, which was roughly halfway between Corinth and the landing. These roads were connected by a number of smaller roads and came together at a point about three miles from the landing. During the day of April 3, according to the march order, the two corps of Hardee and Polk, with Hardee in the lead, were to follow the Ridge Road

## JOHN C. BRECKINRIDGE

Born Kentucky 1821; member of an old and honored Bluegrass family; attended Centre College, the College of New Jersey (now Princeton), and studied law at Transylvania University; practiced law briefly in Lexington in 1845; after a short residence in Iowa, he returned to Kentucky and married Mary Cyrene Birch; despite his family's Whig background, he took an interest in Democratic politics; saw no action during the War with Mexico, but visited Mexico City as major in the 3d Kentucky Volunteers; served in the Kentucky legislature from 1849 to 1851, and in the U.S. House of Representatives from 1851 to 1855; nominated and elected Vice President of the United States on the James Buchanan ticket in 1856, the youngest in American history; in 1859, a year and a half before his term was to expire, he was

until they reached a farmhouse named Mickey's, about seven miles from the landing. Cheatham's Division was to join Polk's Corps on the march by moving from its location at Bethel Station along a road that intersected the Ridge Road shortly before it reached Mickey's.

Meantime, Bragg's Corps was to march to Monterey on the road bearing the village name then proceed on a connecting road to join the other two corps in the vicinity of Mickey's, where the entire army would bivouac for the night. The reserve brigades under Breckinridge would move from Burnsville through the village of Farmington and join the main body at Mickey's.

Although the march to battle followed the general plan set forth in Beauregard's order, it quickly fell into chaos and delay.

elected to the U.S. Senate by the Kentucky legislature; in 1860 accepted presidential nomination of the Southern Rights wing of the split Democratic Party; favored southern rights, and when Kentucky declared for the Union in September 1861, he accepted a commission as Confederate brigadier general; in 1862 promoted to major general, commanded the reserve corps at Shiloh, defended Vicksburg, and failed in an attack on Baton Rouge, but fought desperately at Murfreesboro; in 1863 participated in General Joseph Johnston's Campaign to relieve Vicksburg; in 1864 commanded the Department of Southwest Virginia, winning the Battle of New Market in May, and accompanied General Jubal Early in the raid on Washington; on February 4, 1865, President Davis appointed him secretary of war; following Confederate surrender, he escaped to Cuba, then to England, and finally to Canada; disclaimed all political ambitions, returned to Kentucky, and resumed his law practice. He died in Lexington, Kentucky, in 1875. "What a handsome and imposing appearance he made! Tall, straight, dignified, he was the ideal Kentuckian among Kentuckians," exclaimed a soldier. General Robert E. Lee considered Breckinridge a "lofty, pure, strong man. . . a great man."

Confusion prevailed in Corinth on the morning of the third; the various units had great difficulty even in getting out of the town. Hardee found his column blocked in the streets by Polk's troops and wagons; Hardee was not able to get on the Ridge Road until after noon. He bivouacked his troops on the road and did not reach Mickey's until the following morning, twelve hours late according to the plan.

Bragg was unable to leave Corinth as scheduled and did not reach Monterey until noon of the fourth. Breckinridge did not get his reserve brigades on the road until 3:00 o'clock on the morning of the fourth. Seeing the impossibility of making his attack at any time that day, Johnston met late that afternoon in Monterey with Beauregard and Bragg and reset the attack for the morning of April 5.

Throughout the night of the fourth the troops were subjected to a spring downpour. A soldier who was in the march gave his impressions of it in a letter home. "It was dark as Eribus," he said, "We were drawn up on the edge [of the road]. As we stood there, troops tramped by in the mud and rain, and darkness. . . . To us who were simply standing in line in the rain it was bad enough, but those men who were going by were wading, stumbling and plunging through mud and water a foot deep."

Hardee, whose corps was to lead the attack, was slow in moving into position the morning of the fifth. As his green troops deployed throughout the woods they violated all the rules of secrecy and security. Many discharged their muskets to determine whether the powder had become too wet to fire. Many shot at rabbits scampering among the trees. When a deer sprang up and fled before them, they uttered a shout that was probably audible for miles. Hardee's Corps was not in position to attack until midmorning.

Still Bragg's Corps was not up. One of his divisions was somewhere on the road. Johnston fretted and urged Bragg to hasten his deployment. Finally, shortly after noon, Johnston lost his patience and exclaimed, "This is perfectly puerile! This is not war!" He then called for horses, and he and some of his staff rode back along the road. They found the lost division standing idle on the road, blocked by Polk's artillery and trains. Johnston quickly cleared the road and sent the tardy unit forward. By now the hour had reached 4:00 o'clock in the afternoon. Johnston reset the attack for the early morning of April 6.

To inspire his troops to a supreme effort, Johnston wrote out a brief address to be read to them at breaks on the march and in bivouac prior to the attack. He called upon them to fight to drive out the "agrarian mercenaries" who had been sent to despoil the South of liberty, property, and honor. He spoke of "the precious stake involved" in the war, and of "the fair, broad, abounding land, [and] the happy homes [that would] be desolated. . . by defeat." He told the soldiers that millions of southern eyes rested upon them and that they must show themselves "worthy of their race and lineage [and of] the women of the South." He closed with these words: "With such incentive to brave deeds, and with the trust that God is with us your generals will lead you confidently to the combat, assured of success."

In a further attempt to elevate the morale of his troops and impart to them a full measure of his own confidence and deter-mination, he rode from one unit to another while they were on the march or being deployed for battle. To one group he said, "I am glad to find you in such good spirits. I think we will beat the Yankees out today." To another, "Well boys, look down the muzzles of your guns, and aim low, today you will have warm work to do!" This face-to-face appeal kindled the enthusiasm of the soldiers and caused them to break into cheers at his approach.

The Union army rested between two streams (Owl Creek and Lick Creek), with the camps extending for approximately four miles away from the landing on the river. Beauregard's attack order provided for Hardee's Corps, spread in line from creek to creek, to initiate the operation in the early morning. Bragg's Corps was to follow, arranged in line, a thousand yards behind Hardee. Polk was to deploy in an unspecified formation and move his corps at an unspecified interval behind Bragg; Breckinridge's reserve brigades were to move at an unspecified interval behind Polk. An addendum to the original order directed that the Confederate main effort was to be made on the right, with the object of cutting the Federal army off from Pittsburg Landing and driving it into the Owl Creek bottom to be destroyed.

The formation described in the order was most unusual. The width of the attacking corps lines (approximately three miles) would render control by the corps commanders extremely difficult if not impossible. Even worse, the troops of the various corps would become completely intermingled once all were in action. The more or less even spread of the formation would give no extra weight to the Confederate right, which was supposed to carry the main effort of the attack. Such a formation would tend to drive the Federals back upon the landing instead of cutting them off from it. Finally, by attacking in waves instead of en masse, the Confederates lost much of the advantage of surprise.

Johnston and Beauregard would receive severe and justified criticism for such a cumbersome and ineffectual plan, Beauregard for originating it and Johnston for accepting it. Johnston had indicated in his message to Davis a far superior attack formation, one in which the three main corps would attack abreast, with Polk on the left, Hardee in the center, and Bragg (with the largest of the corps) on the right.

Why and how Johnston's outlined plan was altered remains a mystery. Beauregard said he submitted the plan to Johnston before the march began and that it was accepted without a change. William Preston Johnston maintained that his father received the written order only after the march began and judged the hour too late for a change. The son also believed

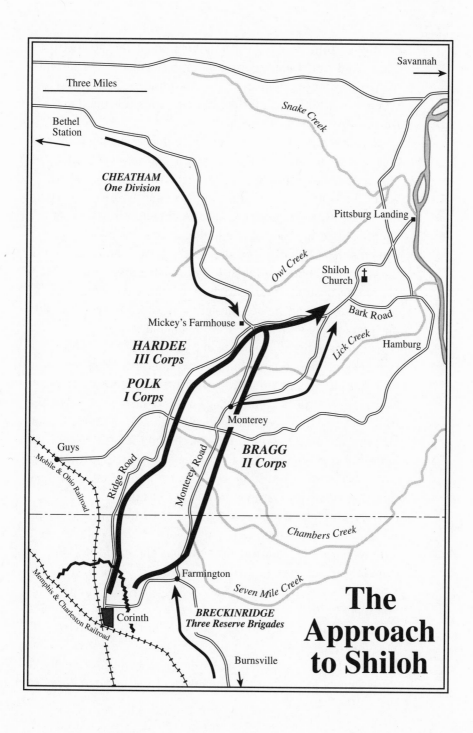

Three Miles

Savannah

Snake Creek

Bethel
Station

CHEATHAM
One Division

Pittsburg Landing

Owl Creek

Shiloh
Church

Bark Road

Mickey's Farmhouse

HARDEE
III Corps

Lick Creek

Hamburg

POLK
I Corps

Monterey

Guys

Ridge Road

Mobile & Ohio Railroad

Monterey Road

BRAGG
II Corps

Chambers Creek

Memphis & Charleston Railroad

Farmington

Seven Mile Creek

Corinth

BRECKINRIDGE
Three Reserve Brigades

Burnsville

# The
# Approach
# to Shiloh

his father told Beauregard how he wished the attack to be made, and that Beauregard deliberately substituted his own plan. The younger Johnston said his father sent Davis a dispatch explaining the matter, but the dispatch disappeared. Davis corroborated this account.

No contemporary documentary evidence surfaced to support the accusation that Beauregard knowingly changed the plan; yet it could possibly have been true. He was a strong-willed and officious person, and he once wrote to a friend before the war, explaining that he had come to believe in the superiority of the English method of attack, in lines instead of columns. It may have been that in the haste and confusion of the occasion Johnston failed to inform Beauregard of the formation he desired. In any event, Johnston knew the nature of the formation well before the battle began; the responsibility for it rests upon him as the army commander.

Hardly was the Confederate army in position to attack when a serious command situation arose. Beauregard lost his nerve and began to say the operation ought to be cancelled. Engaging the corps commanders a short distance behind the front, he insisted that Confederate success depended upon surprise and that delays in the march and the noisiness of the approach had rendered a surprise impossible—that the enemy would be "entrenched to their eyes." He urged that the attack be called off and the army returned to Corinth.

Johnston joined the group and heard Beauregard's expostulations, to which Bragg and the others except Polk, agreed. Johnston was faced with the supreme command decision of the entire campaign; he had reached the "moment of truth" so vividly described by the famed German military analyst Karl von Clausewitz.

Clausewitz wrote that as soon as difficulties arise, the machine itself begins to offer resistance as the resolve of one individual after another breaks down and the inertia of the mass comes to rest on the shoulders of the commander; that he must exercise great force of will in order to overcome the loss of determination among his subordinates; that he is exposed to a constant whirlpool of true and false information and mistakes made either through negligence, willful contravention of authority, or lack of understanding. "In short," wrote Clausewitz, "he is the victim of a hundred thousand impressions, of which the most have an intimidating, the fewest an encouraging tendency. . . . High courage and stability of character stand proof against them as the rock resists the beating of the waves."

Johnston listened quietly to Beauregard and reflected briefly. He said that he still hoped to find the enemy unprepared. Then he announced, "We shall attack at daylight tomorrow."

He spent the night in his headquarters near the Confederate line. As his soldiers slept he and a group of his officers sat for a time around a small campfire and discussed the forthcoming battle. Johnston expressed his confidence of victory. "I believe I will hammer 'em beyond doubt," he said. "Tomorrow at twelve o'clock we will water our horses in the Tennessee River."

After the others left, Johnston remained for a short while at the embers of the dying fire, apparently lost in meditation. Unquestionably, he thought of the coming battle. Perhaps he thought of the countless associates from every stage in his long career who were now soldiers in the army that lay about him, and how many of them would die in the fray. Doubtless his mind turned to his wife and children whom he had left in faraway California. Finally he retired. Tomorrow would be a fateful day.

# 4
## SHILOH

Johnston and his staff were up before dawn on April 6. He was optimistic over the prospect of victory. Prisoners captured the previous evening reported that General Grant had returned to his headquarters in Savannah, thus strengthening Johnston's confidence that the Union commander did not expect an attack. Beauregard nevertheless renewed his objections. The sudden outbreak of firing spared Johnston the necessity of overruling his shaken second-in-command again. Instead, he said simply, "The battle has opened; it is too late to change our dispositions now." He then indicated his intention to accompany the attacking line, leaving Beauregard to man-

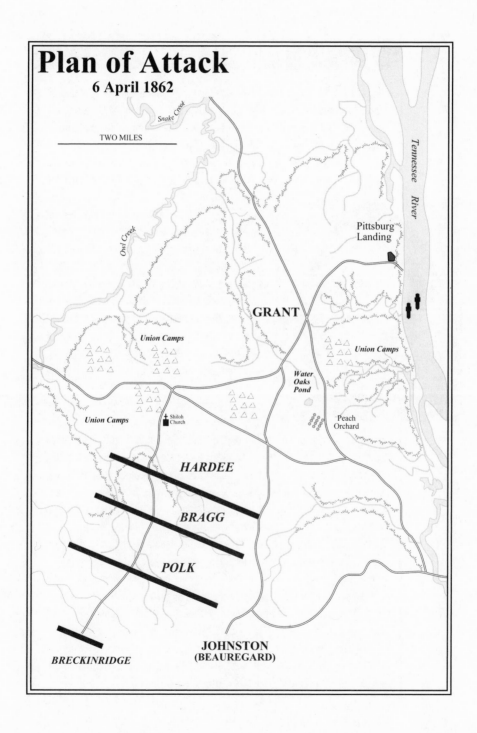

# Plan of Attack
## 6 April 1862

TWO MILES

Snake Creek

Owl Creek

Tennessee River

Pittsburg Landing

GRANT

Union Camps

Union Camps

Water Oaks Pond

Union Camps

✝ Shiloh Church

Peach Orchard

*HARDEE*

*BRAGG*

*POLK*

*BRECKINRIDGE*

**JOHNSTON**
(BEAUREGARD)

## BENJAMIN M. PRENTISS

Born (West) Virginia 1819; as a youth he moved with his family to Missouri, and later settled at Quincy, Illinois, where he served in the militia during the Mormon conflict of the early 1840s; Prentiss then commanded a company of Illinois volunteers in the Mexican War, after which he studied and practiced law in Quincy; entering Republican politics, he lost a bid for the House of Representatives in 1860; with the onset of the Civil War, he entered the

volunteer ranks as a captain in the 10th Illinois, but quickly rose to colonel of the regiment; in August 1861 he was appointed brigadier general of U.S. Volunteers; commanding a large area of northern Missouri, he was charged with quelling secessionist activity in the state; in March 1862 he assumed command of the Sixth Division, Army of the Tennessee; surprised with the rest of General U.S. Grant's force in the Battle of Shiloh, the Sixth Division was sent reeling, but Prentiss rallied elements of the scattered army and mounted a tenacious defense of the so-called Hornets' Nest, buying valuable time for Grant to organize a defense until finally compelled to surrender late in the day; despite his stubborn stand that likely saved Grant's army and the fact that the reenforced Federals won the battle, the captured Prentiss became something of a scapegoat for the humiliating surprise; exchanged in October 1862, he served on the infamous court-martial of General Fitz John Porter; given command of the District of Eastern Arkansas and headquartered at Helena, he was promoted to major general of Volunteers in March 1863; that July he repulsed a Confederate attack on Helena; clearly relegated to a secondary role, he resigned in August, citing health and family concerns; he resumed his law practice in Quincy, and later in Missouri, and also served as a Federal pension agent; he was postmaster at Bethany, Missouri, at the time of his death in 1901. General Prentiss deserved high praise for his stand in the Hornets' Nest; instead he paid for the Federal failures on the first day at Shiloh, while those more to blame—Grant and General William T. Sherman—survived largely unscathed, enabling them eventually to lead the Union to victory.

age the rear echelon of the army, to expedite the movement of troops and supplies to points where they were needed on the front.

Riding forward through his ranks, Johnston greeted the troops with expressions of warmth and encouragement. To a young officer who was a distant relative, "I never see you but I think of William [Preston Johnston]. I hope you may get through safely today, but we must win a victory." To another, "My son, we must this day conquer or perish." To an Arkansas regiment, "Men of Arkansas! They say you boast of your prowess with the bowie knife. Today you wield a nobler weapon—the bayonet. Employ it well." With these and many other words he sought to inspire his soldiers to a superhuman effort.

As the sun rose (some of the troops, recalling one of Napoleon's greatest victories, spoke dramatically of the "sun of Austerlitz") the assaulting wave swept into the outer Union camps, those of Brigadier General Benjamin M. Prentiss's and Major General William T. Sherman's Divisions. The fighting was in the vicinity of a small rural Methodist church named Shiloh, from which the battle would take its name among Southerners. The first truly great engagement of the Civil War had opened.

Johnston quickly observed that he was correct in believing the Union army would not be expecting an attack. The surprise was complete. Grant and Sherman had altogether misinterpreted Confederate capabilities and intentions and grossly neglected the local security of their commands. Johnston had accurately read their minds when he said the afternoon before that he yet expected to find them unprepared. His decision confirmed a principle set forth by Colonel G.F.R. Henderson, an acute contemporary British soldier and military analyst, who said: "If in appearance great risks [are] run, it [is] with the full knowledge that the enemy's character or his apprehensions would prevent him from taking those simple precautions by which the critics point out that the whole enterprise might easily [be] ruined. They [great generals] penetrate . . . their adversary's brain!"

When Johnston reached the front he found Hardee's troops fiercely engaged with the Federals. Seeing one Confederate brigade stopped, Johnston rallied it personally; it pressed forward and drove the Federals into retreat. But observing that the Confederates suffered heavy losses and gained ground slowly, Johnston ordered Bragg's Corps up, and by 7:00 o'clock it was in the line. Later Johnston ordered Polk's Corps into combat, except for one brigade that Beauregard had already committed.

Johnston continued to follow the front and soon halted at two cabins located on the edge of an open field to watch Brigadier General Patrick Cleburne's Arkansas troops deliver a successful charge. Entering a captured Union camp, Johnston rounded up Confederate looters and sent them into action. When Federal prisoners, some speaking only in German, prostrated themselves before him and begged their lives, he replied, "Why men, you don't suppose we kill prisoners, do you? Go [to] the rear & you will be safe there." Meeting here with Hardee, Johnston briefly discussed the situation with him, then rode on to observe another part of the line.

By mid-morning the entire Confederate army, except for two reserve brigades under Breckinridge, was in the fray, as was the entire Union force at Pittsburg Landing. The combat was extraordinarily furious and bloody. One veteran wrote later, "Since [Shiloh] I have been in many pitched battles including Perryville, Murfreesboro, Chickamauga & Franklin, but none ever made the same impression on me." Both Grant and Sherman recalled that the first day at Shiloh was as severe as any other fighting they witnessed in the war.

During most of the morning Johnston covered the front from left to right, talking with corps, division, and brigade commanders, and sometimes with regimental commanders.

Through his staff he sent instructions and received information from all points along the line, and he personally observed the situation and terrain on those parts of the field that he visited.

## WILLIAM T. SHERMAN

Born Ohio 1820; graduated from U.S. Military Academy 1840, sixth in his class; 2d lieutenant 3rd Artillery 1840; 1st lieutenant 1841; stationed in California during Mexican War; captain 1850. Resigned from army 1853 to become banker; after business failed, Sherman voluntarily assumed personal financial responsibility for money lost by his friends; practiced law for a short time in Kansas, losing only case he tried; from 1859 to 1861 superintendent of military college that later became Louisiana State University. Colonel 13th Infantry and then brigadier general volunteers 1861; commanded brigade at First Bull Run; commanded division at Shiloh; major general volunteers 1862 to 1864, serving under Grant in the Vicksburg and Chattanooga campaigns; brigadier general U.S. Army 1863; major general 1864; assumed direction of principal military operations in the West. Directed Meridian and Atlanta campaigns, March to the Sea, and Carolina campaign that ended in surrender of Joseph E. Johnston's army in 1865; received thanks of Congress "for gallant and arduous services" during the Civil War; lieutenant general 1866; general 1869; commander of the army  1869 to 1883; retired 1883; published memoirs 1875; died 1891. Made his famous statement, "war is all hell," in a speech at Columbus, Ohio, in 1880. An officer noted that Sherman's "features express determination, particularly the mouth. He is a very homely man, with a regular nest of wrinkles in his face, which play and twist as he eagerly talks on each subject; but his expression is pleasant and kindly." Some authorities rate him an even better general than Grant.

He soon became aware that although the Confederate left and center were advancing satisfactorily, the right, which was the main effort, was halted by determined Union resistance along a wagon road in the woods and the border of a small peach orchard. The soldiers likened the entire area to a "hornets' nest." At around 9:30, while at another captured Union camp, he received from Captain S.H. Lockett of the engineers a written message and penciled sketch that indicated the location of the Union resistance. Moving into a shallow ravine for protection against bursting shells, he reflected for some time on the message and listened to the sounds of the battle. He knew it was imperative to get his main effort moving.

At 10:20 he dispatched a staff officer to instruct Breckinridge to take his reserve brigades to the right and make his way to the Tennessee River in order to turn the Union left flank. When Lockett reported back to Johnston, and Breckinridge had not appeared, Johnston sent the engineer officer to lead the reserve into position.

As Johnston moved farther right to supervise the operation at this critical point, he rode through another overrun Union camp, where he found himself surrounded by the unattended wounded of both armies. To his personal surgeon, Dr. D.W. Yandell, he said, "Look after these wounded people, the Yankees among the rest. They were our enemies a moment ago. They are prisoners now." When the doctor protested, saying he needed to remain with Johnston, the general promised not to leave the spot without him.

Soon he broke his promise. He probably forgot it. In any event, he rode away to observe and control the attack at the right flank of his line; he gave direction and offered encouragement to every Confederate division commander in that area. All of them attested to the effectiveness of his instructions. He extended Bragg's line to the right in an effort to envelop the Union left flank. When the reserve brigades appeared about noon Johnston committed them to action on his right. He was now attempting to correct the flawed attack formation called for in Beauregard's order.

As the reserves moved up, Johnston said to one commander, "A few more charges and the day [is] ours." This prophecy turned out to be too optimistic. The Union line stretched farther to the left than he had believed it to be; instead of turning the enemy flank, as he had intended, his reserve troops became engaged in the heavy fighting at the peach orchard and beyond toward the river. For two more hours he sought futilely to overwhelm the defenders of this position.

Finally, the assaults began to falter from casualties and fatigue. At approximately 2:00 o'clock General Breckinridge came to him, saying that one of his regiments, the 45th Tennessee Volunteer Infantry, refused to fight any more. After Governor Harris of Tennessee, a member of the staff, failed to persuade the regiment to make another charge, and Breckinridge insisted that he could not do it, Johnston said, "Oh, yes, general, I think you can." He then offered to help Breckinridge in the task.

Riding along the front of the reluctant regiment, Johnston spoke words of encouragement to the soldiers. Touching the points of some of the bayonets, he said, "These will do the work. . . Men, they are stubborn; we must use the bayonet." When he came to the center of the line he suddenly pivoted his horse, Fire Eater, toward the enemy, shouting, "I will lead you." These words and actions rekindled the spirits of the troops; they charged forward in response, drove back the defending Federals, and took their immediate objective.

Eyewitnesses were unclear as to whether Johnston actually led the charge all the way. Perhaps he led it a short distance, then dropped back to the rear. Unquestionably, he was under fire for a time, because a musket ball grazed his thigh, another struck the sole of his boot, and his horse was lightly wounded in two spots. Johnston was delighted over the success of the action. Pointing to his damaged boot, he said to Harris,

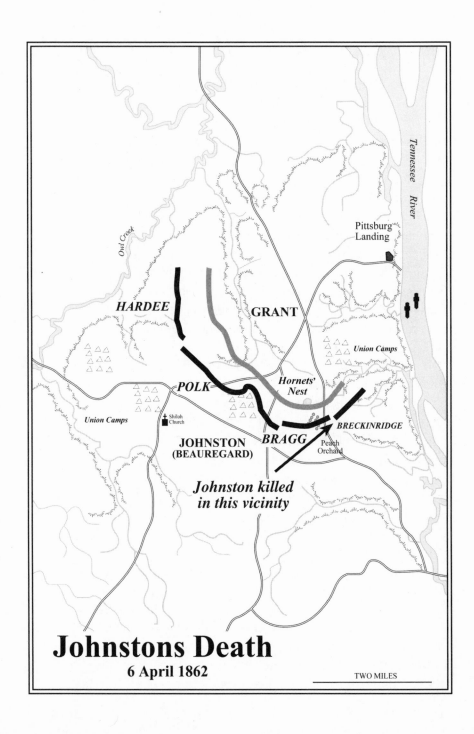

**Johnstons Death**
**6 April 1862**

TWO MILES

"Governor, they came very near putting me hors de combat in that charge."

Suddenly Federal artillery opened fire from the woods beyond the peach orchard. Johnston dispatched Harris to order Colonel W.S. Statham, one of Breckinridge's brigade commanders, to move his unit to the left and silence the battery. Harris dashed away and delivered the order. He returned to discover Johnston reeling unsteadily in his saddle. Harris cried, "General, are you wounded?" Johnston replied deliberately, "Yes, and I fear seriously." Harris put his arm about Johnston and, assisted by Captain W.L. Wickham, directed their horses down into an adjacent wooded ravine, where they laid him on the ground and began to search his body for the wound.

They failed to find one, although he was bleeding profusely from a torn artery in his right leg just below the knee where a bullet had struck him. Possibly his attendants were blinded by panic; possibly the blood drained into his boot and could not be seen.

Other members of his staff arrived. They attempted to stimulate him with brandy and whiskey. There was no response. Colonel William Preston, his brother-in-law and a member of his staff, knelt beside him and addressed him, "Johnston, don't you know me?" Again, no response. Finally, Colonel Dudley Haydon, another staff officer, felt his chest and said he could detect no heartbeat. "My God," cried Preston. "My God. Haydon, is it so?" It was so. Albert Sidney Johnston was dead.

He died of loss of blood through the ruptured leg artery. If he had kept his promise to Dr. Yandell, the physician probably would have saved him by locating the wound and applying a tourniquet which, ironically, Johnston had in his pocket. His act of compassion for the wounded soldiers of both sides had perhaps cost him his life.

As soon as the shocked staff realized that Johnston was dead they wrapped his body in a blanket and carried it back to

Beauregard's headquarters. Beauregard took command of the army and ordered that the news of Johnston's death be concealed from the troops because of the demoralizing effect it would produce among them.

Beauregard also ordered that the Confederate attack be continued. It was continued, though a significant lapse occurred following Johnston's death. Late in the afternoon the Federal commander in the Hornets' Nest, General Prentiss,

## WILLIAM PRESTON

Born Kentucky 1816; he received a law degree from Harvard in 1838 and opened a practice in Louisville; during the Mexican War he served as lieutenant colonel of a Kentucky regiment; following the war, he served in both houses of the Kentucky legislature and in 1852 was elected to the U. S. House of Representatives, serving two terms; in 1858 he was appointed minister to Spain by President James Buchanan; upon his return to the U. S., he became a leading advocate of Kentucky secession; following the outbreak of the Civil War, Preston joined his brother-in-law General Albert Sidney Johnston at Bowling Green, Kentucky; appointed colonel and assigned to the staff of General John C. Breckinridge, he served in that capacity through the Battle of Shiloh in April 1862; promoted to brigadier general, he led a brigade at Corinth, Murfreesboro, and Chickamauga; in January 1864, whether owing to his diplomatic skill or his open criticism of General Braxton Bragg, Preston was appointed minister to Mexico; unable to reach Emperor Maximilian, he spent the balance of the war in the Trans-Mississippi; following the war, he traveled to Mexico, England, and Canada before returning to Kentucky in 1866; he served two more terms in the state house and remained active in Democratic politics; General Preston died at Lexington in 1887.

finding his unit surrounded, capitulated to the Confederates. Two of Bragg's brigades approached Pittsburg Landing but were repulsed by fire from massed artillery that had been assembled for the protection of the Union base. Shortly after 6:00 o'clock Beauregard ordered the attack halted and the forward Confederate troops withdrawn in order to give them a night's rest. He indicated that the battle would be resumed the following morning.

Beauregard erred badly in these decisions. He issued the order to halt the fighting without conferring with any of his corps commanders or personally observing the situation on the front. Either he should have pressed the battle to the utmost on the first day, or he should have retreated to Corinth that night. At the end of the day Grant's army was reinforced by one of its divisions (Major General Lew Wallace's) that had been absent during the battle and by one brigade of Buell's force; during the night the main body of Buell's army arrived. Beauregard's behavior exposed his army to the threat of destruction.

When fighting began on April 7 the Union army outnumbered the Confederates by approximately two to one. That afternoon Beauregard, seeing that his army was nearing collapse, broke off the action and retreated to Corinth. Thus the great western campaign ended in Confederate defeat at Shiloh.

The Union tactical victory at Shiloh was also a major strategic victory in that it left a powerful army poised for the invasion of the lower Mississippi Valley. But even in defeat the Confederacy also reaped significant strategic benefits from the battle. It was so bloody with its almost 25,000 casualties (3,500 of them dead), so stunning to Grant's mind that he made no serious effort to pursue and destroy the badly crippled Confederate army, and so stunning to Halleck's mind that he made no serious immediate effort to continue the penetration of the lower Mississippi Valley. Shiloh gained months of precious time for the Confederacy in the West.

# 5
## ASSESSMENT OF A GENERAL

Johnston's death left two important questions unanswered. What would have been the outcome of the Battle of Shiloh if he had not been killed? And, how good a general was he?

The prevailing opinion on Shiloh is that his death did not alter the outcome of the battle. This, however, is conjectural. Because Beauregard did not win the battle does not prove that Johnston could not have won it. His orders and conduct at the key point of the battlefield meant something quite different from Beauregard's efforts from far behind the front. The Confederates were advancing before Johnston fell; his spirits were high. Alive and galvanized by the prospect of victory, he might well have achieved it.

No determined Confederate move occurred immediately following Johnston's death; the Confederate attack faltered seriously. Accounts of the battle written by participants, both Confederate and Union, indicate a definite break in the fighting at that time. Bragg's official report, prepared a few days after the engagement, long before any controversy had arisen over the issue, and by the officer who was in the best position to know the situation on the field, is especially clear and forceful on this point. He wrote, "No one cause probably contributed so greatly to our loss of time, which was the loss of success, as the fall of the commanding general. For want of a common superior to the different commands on that part of the field, great delay occurred after this misfortune, and that delay prevented the consummation of the work so gallantly and successfully begun."

A powerful voice from the other side lent support to Bragg's conclusion. General Sherman wrote in his memoirs, "There was [following Johnston's death] a perceptible lull for a couple of hours, when the attack was renewed, but with much less vehemence, and continued up to dark."

Additionally, the battle report of Brigadier General Stephen A. Hurlbut, commander of a Federal division on the critical left flank of the Hornets' Nest, offered strong circumstantial evidence of a suspension in the fighting there. Hurlbut's Division withdrew from the line at about 3:00 p.m. in order to help form the historic final defensive perimeter in front of Pittsburg Landing. The commander's narrative showed unmistakably that the withdrawal was feasible only because his sector was no longer under attack. Writing after the war, Hurlbut declined to comment on the reason for this development, but admitted that he "was exceedingly grateful for the cause be it what it might, which gave us abundant time to take up a new position & prepare to hold it to the death." Unanswered is the question: would Johnston have permitted this abundant time?

Johnston died too early in the war for the question concerning the quality of his generalship to be fully answered. The answer is further complicated by the unusual relationship between him and his second-in-command Beauregard. Many students of the war accept Beauregard's claim that he was the architect of the Confederate strategy that culminated in the Battle of Shiloh and the actual commander of the Confederate army in the battle; that Johnston was a mere shadow commander.

Johnston respected Beauregard and valued his advice and support. Beauregard was sensitive in matters of protocol, and quicker than Johnston in thought and word. Consequently, Johnston deferred to him in matters of form. At Bowling Green, the important Covington House conference occurred in Beauregard's headquarters; at Corinth, Johnston offered him the field command, had him draft the plan for the organization of the army, instructed the corps commanders to report directly to him, and delegated to him the preparation of the march and attack orders.

In matters of content, however, Johnston made all of the major strategic, operational, and tactical decisions. Most of those made prior to the battle were made with Beauregard's concurrence, but significantly, the supreme decision, that the attack be carried out, had to be made over Beauregard's vehement objections. In making this decision, Johnston demonstrated superior attributes of will, decisiveness, presence of mind, and ability to evaluate his opponent.

During the climactic battle, in addition to inspiring his soldiers with his presence, Johnston personally committed the vast majority of them (perhaps ninety percent) to action, located the critical point of Federal resistance, and directed the attack of his reserves against it at the moment and in the manner of his choosing. He was the real commander of the Confederate army at all times.

Johnston has been criticized for placing himself where he was vulnerable to enemy fire. Some have said he should have remained at a safe distance behind the line, commanding through his staff and aides; that he was out of touch with the battle as a whole. But he was not, in fact, out of touch with the battle. He used his staff to maximal effect, dispatching staff

## STEPHEN A. HURLBUT

Born South Carolina 1815; Hurlbut studied law and was admitted to the South Carolina bar, opening a practice in Charleston; he served as adjutant in a South Carolina militia regiment in actions against the Seminoles in Florida; in 1845 he relocated to Belvidere, Illinois, where he became active in politics; a leading Republican in the state legislature at the outbreak of the Civil War, in June 1861 he was appointed brigadier general of U.S. Volunteers by President Abraham Lincoln; he commanded the Fourth Division, Army of the Tennessee, in the Battle of Shiloh and at Corinth, but for the bulk of the war he held largely administrative, rear-area positions in the far-flung Army of the Tennessee, mostly in the Memphis area; in this capacity, he supported operations against Vicksburg; from December 1862 to April 1864, he commanded the Sixteenth Corps, Army of the Tennessee; in the meantime he received promotion in September 1862 to major general, U.S.V.; transferred to command the Department of the Gulf in September 1864, Hurlbut exploited his position for personal financial gain and engaged in other corrupt practices, for which he was charged; General E.R.S. Canby ordered his arrest and trial, but the case was quashed and the embattled general was honorably mustered out of the Volunteers in June 1865;

returning to Belvidere, he resumed his political career and became the first head of the Grand Army of the Republic; despite persistent allegations of corruption and drunkenness, he was appointed minister to Colombia by President U.S. Grant; in 1872 he was elected to the first of two terms in the U.S. House of Representatives; appointed minister to Peru by President James Garfield in 1881, he again was charged with mismanagement and financial impropriety. General Hurlbut died on duty in Lima, Peru, in 1882.

officers to collect information and to deliver orders and instructions. Ironically, not a member of his staff was with him when he was mortally wounded.

Certainly, leading a regiment is not the proper role of a commanding general; doubtless Johnston exposed himself too recklessly on that one critical occasion. Yet there is cause to believe that he understood the situation of the Confederate army better and communicated his orders more effectively than if he had been somewhere in the rear. When he spoke to his subordinates eye-to-eye, they comprehended precisely what he meant; when they spoke to him eye-to-eye he comprehended precisely what they meant.

In addition to his other insights, Johnston was aware that his ability to fire his troops to a supreme effort was fully as important to victory as his decisions and orders in the field, and that his presence at the front was required to accomplish this end. As a motivator he was virtually without peer. That his friends and admirers attested to this quality comes as no surprise, but so did those officers who previously had lost confidence in him. Hardee believed that the Confederates would have won the contest at Shiloh had he remained alive. Gilmer wrote, "He devoted talents of the highest order, energies unceasing, and a singleness of purpose never equalled."

Even those subordinates who later became severe critics of Johnston applauded his leadership at the time. Colonel Jordan wrote immediately after the war, that Johnston "stimulated the onslaught by his personal presence on the right." Beauregard wrote in his report of the battle that Johnston "showed the highest qualities of the commander, and a personal intrepidity that inspired all around him, and gave resistless impulsion to his columns at critical moments." Johnston's electric presence at the front added a potent weapon to the Confederate attack.

He made a number of serious miscalculations and mistakes of judgment during his brief Civil War career. But in the climax of that career, he rose above all others engaged in the war, both Confederate and Union. One might question what Beauregard's reputation would be today if he had been killed at mid-afternoon of April 6 after having lost his nerve for the attack; or what Grant's or Sherman's reputations would have been after grossly misreading the strategic situation and being taken by utter surprise in the engagement. These other commanders had opportunities to grow with experience as the war went on. Although death robbed Johnston of such an opportunity, he had already demonstrated a genuine capacity for growth.

Without doubt, if he had lived to win a decisive victory at Shiloh, as he might have done, he would have been hailed as the Confederacy's preeminent soldier. Even short of a complete victory there he would have emerged as a general of towering character, unshakable determination, and dauntless spirit who was capable of anticipating and out-thinking his opponents, and as a troop leader of unsurpassed inspirational qualities in battle. He might have done for the Western Theater of the war what Lee did for the Eastern Theater. Jefferson Davis had reason to consider Johnston his greatest general.

# AFTERWORD

Johnston's body was embalmed at Beauregard's headquarters on the field. Johnston's staff then bore the body by wagon back to Corinth, where it was bathed and dressed for burial. From Corinth, they took it by train to New Orleans to be interred, at the invitation of Mayor John T. Monroe, in the Monroe family tomb in the St. Louis Cemetery. The body lay there for almost five years.

But Johnston's closest ties of sentiment were with Texas, where he had spent much of his career. He was quoted by family members as having said that when he died he wished a handful of Texas earth to be scattered upon his breast. Hence, when in the fall of 1866 the Texas legislature requested his body, the family consented.

The following winter the body was removed with appropriate ceremonies from the New Orleans tomb and buried in the Texas State Cemetery in Austin. Placed atop his final tomb in 1905 is a recumbent marble statue of him produced by the German-born Texas sculptress Elisabet Ney.

Johnston doubtless would have approved of Austin as his

permanent resting place. Upon first seeing the site in 1839 he said it was located "in the finest climate and most beautiful country that the 'blazing eye' of the sun looks upon in his journey from the east to the west."

# APPENDIX A

# ORGANIZATION OF CONFEDERATE FORCES DURING THE BATTLE OF SHILOH APRIL 6-7, 1862

## ARMY OF THE MISSISSIPPI

### GENERAL ALBERT SIDNEY JOHNSTON (killed)
### GENERAL P. G. T. BEAUREGARD

## FIRST ARMY CORPS

MAJ. GEN. LEONIDAS POLK

FIRST DIVISION

BRIG. GEN. CHARLES CLARK (WOUNDED)
BRIG. GEN. ALEXANDER P. STEWART

*FIRST BRIGADE*
COL. ROBERT RUSSELL
*11th Louisiana*
*12th Tennessee*
*13th Tennessee*
*22d Tennessee*
*Bankhead's Tennessee Battery*

*SECOND BRIGADE*
BRIG. GEN. ALEXANDER P. STEWART
*13th Arkansas*
*4th Tennessee*
*5th Tennessee*
*33d Tennessee*
*Stanford's Mississippi Battery*

SECOND DIVISION
MAJ. GEN. BENJAMIN F. CHEATHAM

*FIRST BRIGADE*
BRIG. GEN. BUSHROD R. JOHNSON (WOUNDED)
COL. PRESTON SMITH (WOUNDED)
*Blythe's Mississippi Battalion*
*2d Tennessee*
*15th Tennessee*
*154th Tennessee (senior)*
*Polk's Tennessee Battery*

*SECOND BRIGADE*
COL. WILLIAM STEPHENS
COL. GEORGE MANEY
*7th Kentucky*
*1st Tennessee (battalion)*
*6th Tennessee*
*9th Tennessee*
*Smith's Mississippi Battery*

CAVALRY
*1st Mississippi*
*Mississippi and Alabama Battalion*

*UNATTACHED*
*47th Tennessee Infantry*

# SECOND ARMY CORPS

## MAJ. GEN. BRAXTON BRAGG

### ESCORT
*ALABAMA CAVALRY*

### FIRST DIVISION
### BRIG. GEN. DANIEL RUGGLES

*FIRST BRIGADE*
COL. RANDALL L. GIBSON
*1st Arkansas*
*4th Louisiana*
*13th Louisiana*
*19th Louisiana*

*SECOND BRIGADE*
Brig. Gen. Patton Anderson
*1st Florida Battalion*
*17th Louisiana*
*20th Louisiana*
*9th Texas*
*Confederate Guards Response Battalion*
*5th Company, Washington (Louisiana) Artillery*

*THIRD BRIGADE*
Col. Preston Pond, Jr.
*16th Louisiana*
*18th Louisiana*
*Crescent (La.) Regiment*
*Orleans Guard Battalion*
*38th Tennessee*
*Ketchum's Alabama Battery*

CAVALRY
*Alabama Battalion*

SECOND DIVISION
BRIG. GEN. JONES M. WITHERS

*FIRST BRIGADE*
Brig. Gen. Adley H. Gladden (killed)
Col. Daniel Adams (wounded)
Col. Zach. C. Deas (wounded)
*21st Alabama*
*22d Alabama*
*25th Alabama*
*26th Alabama*
*1st Louisiana*
*Robertson's Alabama Battery*

*SECOND BRIGADE*
Brig. Gen. James R. Chalmers
*5th Mississippi*
*7th Mississippi*
*9th Mississippi*
*10th Mississippi*
*52d Tennessee*
*Gage's Alabama Battery*

*THIRD BRIGADE*
BRIG. GEN. JOHN K. JACKSON
*17th Alabama*
*18th Alabama*
*19th Alabama*
*2d Texas*
*Girardey's Georgia Battery*

# THIRD ARMY CORPS

## MAJ. GEN. WILLIAM J. HARDEE (WOUNDED)

*FIRST BRIGADE*
BRIG. GEN. THOMAS C. HINDMAN (ALSO COMMANDED THIRD BRIGADE)
COL. R. G. SHAVER
*2d Arkansas*
*6th Arkansas*
*7th Arkansas*
*3d Confederate*
*Swett's Mississippi Battery*

*SECOND BRIGADE*
BRIG. GEN. PATRICK R. CLEBURNE
*15th Arkansas*
*6th Mississippi*
*2d Tennessee*
*5th [35th] Tennessee*
*23d Tennessee*
*24th Tennessee*
*Trigg's Arkansas Battery*
*Calvert's Arkansas Battery*

*THIRD BRIGADE*
BRIG. GEN. STERLING A. M. WOOD
COL. WILLIAM K. PATTERSON (TEMPORARILY)
*16th Alabama*
*8th Arkansas*
*9th [14th] Arkansas (battalion)*
*27th Tennessee*

*44th Tennessee*
*55th Tennessee*
*Harper's Mississippi Battery*
*Georgia Dragoons (company)*

# RESERVE CORPS

## BRIG. GEN. JOHN C. BRECKINRIDGE

*FIRST BRIGADE*
COL. ROBERT P. TRABUE
*4th Alabama Battalion*
*31st Alabama*
*3d Kentucky*
*4th Kentucky*
*5th Kentucky*
*6th Kentucky*
*Tennessee Battalion (Crew's)*
*Byrne's Kentucky Battery*
*Cobb's Kentucky Battery*
*Kentucky Cavalry (squadron)*

*SECOND BRIGADE*
BRIG. GEN. JOHN S. BOWEN (WOUNDED)
COL. JOHN D. MARTIN
*9th Arkansas*
*10th Arkansas*
*2d Confederate*
*1st Missouri*
*Hudson's Mississippi Battery*

*THIRD BRIGADE*
COL. WINFIELD S. STATHAM
*15th Mississippi*
*22d Mississippi*
*19th Tennessee*
*20th Tennessee*
*28th Tennessee*
*45th Tennessee*
*Rutledge's Tennessee Battery*

*UNATTACHED*

CAVALRY
*Tennessee Regiment (Forrest's)*
*Alabama Regiment (Clanton's)*
*Texas Regiment (Wharton's)*

ARTILLERY
*Hubbard's Arkansas Battery*
*McClung's Tennessee Battery*

# APPENDIX B

## ORGANIZATION OF UNION FORCES DURING THE BATTLE OF SHILOH APRIL 6-7, 1862

## ARMY OF THE TENNESSEE

MAJ. GEN. ULYSSES S. GRANT

FIRST DIVISION
MAJ. GEN. JOHN A. McCLERNAND

*FIRST BRIGADE*
COL. ABRAHAM HARE (WOUNDED)
COL. MARCELLUS CROCKER
*8th Illinois*
*18th Illinois*
*11th Iowa*
*13th Iowa*
*2d Illinois Light Artillery, Battery D*

*SECOND BRIGADE*
COL. C. CARROLL MARSH (ALSO COMMANDED THIRD BRIGADE)
*11th Illinois*
*20th Illinois*
*45th Illinois*
*48th Illinois*

*THIRD BRIGADE*
COL. JULIUS RAITH (MORTALLY WOUNDED)
LT. COL. ENOS P. WOOD
*17th Illinois*
*29th Illinois*
*43d Illinois*
*49th Illinois*
*Illinois Cavalry Company*

*UNATTACHED*
*Stewart's Company, Illinois Cavalry*
*1st Illinois Light Artillery, Battery D*
*2d Illinois Light Artillery, Battery E*
*Ohio Light Artillery, 14th Battery*

SECOND DIVISION
BRIG. GEN. WILLIAM H. L. WALLACE (MORTALLY WOUNDED)
COL. JAMES M. TUTTLE

*FIRST BRIGADE*
COL. JAMES TUTTLE
*2d Iowa*
*7th Iowa*
*12th Iowa*
*14th Iowa*

*SECOND BRIGADE*
BRIG. GEN. JOHN MCARTHUR (WOUNDED)
COL. THOMAS MORTON
*9th Illinois*
*12th Illinois*
*13th Missouri*
*14th Missouri*
*81st Ohio*

*THIRD BRIGADE*
COL. THOMAS W. SWEENY (WOUNDED)
COL. SILAS D. BALDWIN
*8th Iowa*
*7th Illinois*
*50th Illinois*
*52d Illinois*
*57th Illinois*
*58th Illinois*

CAVALRY
*2d Illinois, Company A*
*2d Illinois, Company B*
*2d United States, Company C*
*4th United States, Company I*

ARTILLERY
*1st Illinois Light, Battery A*
*1st Missouri Light, Battery D*
*1st Missouri Light, Battery H*
*1st Missouri Light, Battery K*

THIRD DIVISION
MAJ. GEN. LEWIS WALLACE

*FIRST BRIGADE*
COL. MORGAN SMITH
*11th Indiana*
*24th Indiana*
*8th Missouri*

*SECOND BRIGADE*
COL. JAMES M. THAYER
*23d Indiana*
*1st Nebraska*
*58th Ohio*
*68th Ohio*

*THIRD BRIGADE*
COL. CHARLES WHITTLESEY
*20th Ohio*
*56th Ohio*
*76th Ohio*
*78th Ohio*

ARTILLERY
*Indiana Light, 9th Battery*
*1st Missouri Light, Battery I*

CAVALRY
*11th Indiana, 3d Battalion*
*5th Ohio, 3d Battalion*

FOURTH DIVISION
BRIG. GEN. STEPHEN HURLBUT

*FIRST BRIGADE*
COL. NELSON G. WILLIAMS (WOUNDED)
COL. ISAAC C. PUGH
*28TH Illinois*
*32d Illinois*
*41st Illinois*
*3d Iowa*

*SECOND BRIGADE*
COL. JAMES C. VEATCH
*14TH Illinois*
*15th Illinois*
*46th Illinois*
*25th Indiana*

*THIRD BRIGADE*
BRIG. GEN. JACOB G. LAUMAN
*31st Indiana*
*44th Indiana*
*17th Kentucky*
*25th Kentucky*

CAVALRY
*5th Ohio, 1st and 2d Battalions*

ARTILLERY
*Michigan Light, 2d Battery*
*Missouri Light, Mann's Battery*
*Ohio Light, 13th Battery*

FIFTH DIVISION
BRIG. GEN. WILLIAM T. SHERMAN (WOUNDED)

*FIRST BRIGADE*
COL. JAMES A. MCDOWELL
*40th Illinois*
*6th Iowa*
*46th Ohio*
*Indiana Light Artillery, 6th Battery*

*SECOND BRIGADE*
COL. DAVID STUART (WOUNDED)
LT. COL. OSCAR MALMBORG (TEMPORARILY)
COL. T. KILBY SMITH
*55th Illinois*
*54th Ohio*
*71st Ohio*

*THIRD BRIGADE*
COL. JESSE HILDEBRAND
*53d Ohio*
*57th Ohio*
*77th Ohio*

*FOURTH BRIGADE*
COL. RALPH P. BUCKLAND
*48th Ohio*
*70th Ohio*
*72d Ohio*

CAVALRY
*4th Illinois, 1st and 2d Battalions*

ARTILLERY
MAJ. EZRA TAYLOR
*1st Illinois Light, Battery B*
*1st Illinois Light, Battery E*

SIXTH DIVISION
BRIG. GEN. BENJAMIN M. PRENTISS (CAPTURED)

*FIRST BRIGADE*
COL. EVERETT PEABODY (KILLED)
*12th Michigan*
*21st Missouri*
*25th Missouri*
*16th Wisconsin*

*SECOND BRIGADE*
COL. MADISON MILLER (CAPTURED)
*61st Illinois*
*16th Iowa*
*18th Missouri*

CAVALRY
*11th Illinois (eight companies)*

ARTILLERY
*Minnesota Light, 1st Battery*
*Ohio Light, 5th Battery*

UNATTACHED INFANTRY
*15th Iowa*
*23d Missouri*
*18th Wisconsin*

UNASSIGNED TROOPS
*15th Michigan*
*14th Wisconsin*
*1st Illinois Light Artillery, Battery H*
*1st Illinois Light Artillery, Battery I*
*2d Illinois Light Artillery, Battery B*
*2d Illinois Light Artillery, Battery F*
*Ohio Light Artillery, 8th Battery*

# ARMY OF THE OHIO

MAJ. GEN. DON CARLOS BUELL

SECOND DIVISION
BRIG. GEN. ALEXANDER McD. McCOOK

*FOURTH BRIGADE*
BRIG. GEN. LOVELL H. ROUSSEAU
*6th Indiana*
*5th Kentucky*
*1st Ohio*
*15th United States, 1st Battalion*
*16th United States, 1st Battalion*
*19th United States, 1st Battalion*

*FIFTH BRIGADE*
COL. EDWARD N. KIRK (WOUNDED)
*34th Illinois*
*29th Indiana*
*30th Indiana*
*77th Pennsylvania*

*SIXTH BRIGADE*
COL. WILLIAM GIBSON
*32d Indiana*
*39th Indiana*
*15th Ohio*
*49th Ohio*

ARTILLERY
*5th United States, Battery H*

FOURTH DIVISION
BRIG. GEN. WILLIAM NELSON

*TENTH BRIGADE*
COL. JACOB AMMEN
*36th Indiana*
*6th Ohio*
*24th Ohio*

*NINETEENTH BRIGADE*
COL. WILLIAM B. HAZEN
*9th Indiana*
*6th Kentucky*
*41st Ohio*

*TWENTY-SECOND BRIGADE*
COL. SANDERS D. BRUCE
*1st Kentucky*
*2d Kentucky*
*20th Kentucky*

CAVALRY
*2d Indiana*

FIFTH DIVISION
BRIG. GEN. THOMAS L. CRITTENDEN

*ELEVENTH BRIGADE*
BRIG. GEN. JEREMIAH T. BOYLE
*9th Kentucky*
*13th Kentucky*
*19th Ohio*
*59th Ohio*

*FOURTEENTH BRIGADE*
COL. WILLIAM SOOY SMITH
*11th Kentucky*
*26th Kentucky*
*13th Ohio*

ARTILLERY
*1st Ohio Light, Battery G*
*4th United States, Batteries H and M*

CAVALRY
*3d Kentucky*

SIXTH DIVISION
BRIG. GEN. THOMAS J. WOOD

*TWENTIETH BRIGADE*
BRIG. GEN. JAMES A. GARFIELD
*13th Michigan*
*64th Ohio*
*65th Ohio*

*TWENTY-FIRST BRIGADE*
COL. GEORGE D. WAGNER
*15th Indiana*
*40th Indiana*
*57th Indiana*
*24th Kentucky*

## SELECTED BIBLIOGRAPHY

Connelly, Thomas L. *Army of the Heartland: The Army of Tennessee, 1861-1862*. Baton Rouge: Louisiana State University Press, 1967.

Daniel, Larry J. *Shiloh: The Battle That Changed the War*. New York: Simon & Schuster, 1997.

Davis, Jefferson. *Rise and Fall of the Confederate Government*. 2 vols. New York: Thomas Yoseloff, 1881.

Davis, William C. *Breckinridge: Statesman, Soldier, Symbol*. Baton Rouge: Louisiana State University Press, 1974.

_____. *Jefferson Davis: The Man and his Hour*. New York: HarperCollins, 1991.

Foote, Shelby. *The Civil War, A Narrative: Fort Sumter to Perryville*. New York: Random House, 1958.

Grant, Ulysses S. *Personal Memoirs of U.S. Grant*. 2 vols. New York: Charles A. Webster & Co., 1885.

Hughes, Nathaniel Cheairs, Jr. *General William J. Hardee, Old Reliable*. Baton Rouge: Louisiana State University Press, 1965.

Johnston, William P. *The Life of Gen. Albert Sidney Johnston*. New York: Da Capo Press, 1997.

Jones, Archer. *Confederate Strategy from Shiloh to Vicksburg*. Baton Rouge: Louisiana State University Press, 1961

Losson, Cristopher. *Tennessee's Forgotten Warriors: Frank Cheatham and His Confederate Division*. Knoxville: University of Tennessee Press, 1989.

Martin, David G. *The Shiloh Campaign: March-April, 1862*. New York: Fairfax Press, 1987.

McDonough, James L. *Shiloh, In Hell Before Night*. Knoxville: University of Tennessee Press, 1977.

McWhiney, Grady. *Braxton Bragg and Confederate Defeat*. New York: Columbia University Press, 1969.

Nevin, David. *The Road to Shiloh: Early Battles in the West*. Alexandria, Virginia: Time Life Books, 1983.

Parks, Joseph H. *General Leonidas Polk, C.S.A., the Fighting Bishop.* Baton Rouge: Louisiana State University Press, 1964.

Roland, Charles P. *Albert Sidney Johnston: Soldier of Three Republics.* Austin: University of Texas Press,1964.

Roman, Alfred. *The Military Operations of General Beauregard.* 2 vols. New York: Da Capo Press, 1994.

Shea, William. *War in the West: Pea Ridge and Prairie Grove.* Abilene, Texas: McWhiney Foundation Press, 1996.

Sherman, William T. *Memoirs of General William T. Sherman.* 2 vols. Bloomington: Indiana University Press, 1957.

Simpson, Harold B. *Cry Comanche: the 2nd U.S. Cavalry in Texas: 1855-1861.* Hillsboro, Texas: Hill College Press, 1988.

Sword, Wiley. *Shiloh: Bloody April.* New York: Morrow, 1974.

Williams, T. Harry. *P.G.T. Beauregard: Napoleon in Gray.* Baton Rouge: Louisiana State University Press, 1954.

Woodworth, Steven E. *Jefferson Davis and his Generals: The Failure of Confederate Command in the West.* Lawrence: University Press of Kansas, 1991.

## ABOUT THE BIOGRAPHICAL SKETCHES

The biographical sketches that accompany the photographs in this volume were derived from numerous sources and written by David Coffey and Grady McWhiney.

## SELECTED REFERENCE WORKS

Boatner, Mark M, III. *The Civil War Dictionary.* Revised edition. New York: David McKay Company, 1988.

Current, Richard N. ed. *Encyclopedia of the Confederacy.* 4 vols. New York: Simon & Schuster, 1993.

Davis, William C. ed. *The Confederate General.* 6 vols. National Historical Society, 1991.

Sifakis, Stewart. *Who Was Who in the Union.* New York: Facts on File, 1988.

_____. *Who Was Who in the Confederacy.* New York: Facts on File, 1988.

Warner, Ezra. *Generals in Gray: Lives of the Confederate Commanders.* Baton Rouge: Louisiana State University Press, 1959.

_____. *Generals in Blue: Lives of the Union Commanders.* Baton Rouge: Louisiana State University Press, 1964.

## PHOTO CREDITS

We gratefully acknowledge the assistance of the Library of Congress for the photographs of P.G.T. Beauregard, Braxton Bragg, Simon Bolivar Buckner, Ulysses S. Grant, Isham Harris, William Preston, and William T. Sherman.

We appreciate the cooperation of the U.S. Army History Institute at Carlisle Barracks, Pennsylvania for the photographs of John C. Breckinridge, Jefferson Davis, William J. Hardee, and Leonidas Polk.

We credit the National Archives for the photograph of Albert Sidney Johnston and the Museum of the Confederacy in Richmond, Virginia for the photograph of William Preston Johnston.

The photographs of D.C. Buell, Stephen A. Hurlbut, and Benjamin M. Prentiss are from *Generals in Blue: Lives of the Union Commanders*, by Ezra J. Warner (Louisiana State University Press, 1964.

# INDEX